brilliant
selection
test results

Books to make you better

Books to make you better. To make you *be* better, *do* better, *feel* better. Whether you want to upgrade your personal skills or change your job, whether you want to improve your managerial style, become a more powerful communicator, or be stimulated and inspired as you work.

Prentice Hall Business is leading the field with a new breed of skills, careers and development books. Books that are a cut above the mainstream – in topic, content and delivery – with an edge and verve that will make you better, with less effort.

Books that are as sharp and smart as you are.

Prentice Hall Business.
We work harder – so you don't have to.

For more details on products, and to contact us, visit
www.business-minds.com
www.yourmomentum.com

brilliant
selection
test results

Tests you might have to sit
and how to prepare for them

Susan Hodgson

London ● New York ● Toronto ● Sydney ● Tokyo ● Singapore ● Hong Kong ● Cape Town
New Delhi ● Madrid ● Paris ● Amsterdam ● Munich ● Milan ● Stockholm

PEARSON EDUCATION LIMITED

Head Office:
Edinburgh Gate
Harlow CM20 2JE
Tel: +44 (0)1279 623623
Fax: +44 (0)1279 431059

London Office:
128 Long Acre
London WC2E 9AN
Tel: +44 (0)20 7447 2000
Fax: +44 (0)20 7447 2170
Website: www.business-minds.com
www.yourmomentum.com

First published in Great Britain in 2003

ISBN 0 273 66165 5

British Library Cataloguing in Publication Data
A CIP catalogue record for this book can be obtained from the British Library.

10 9 8 7 6 5 4 3 2 1

Typeset by Northern Phototypesetting Co. Ltd, Bolton
Printed and bound in Great Britain by Bell & Bain Ltd, Glasgow

The Publishers' policy is to use paper manufactured from sustainable forests.

Contents

Acknowledgements

Saville and Holdsworth is a company which develops and publishes an extensive range of psychometric tests and they have kindly provided some verbal, numerical and diagrammatic sample test material which can be found in Part 2 of this book.

David Singmaster is a professor of mathematics and a metagrobologist with much experience of setting mathematical brain teasers and he has kindly provided some challenging and entertaining problems, which can also be found in Part 2 of this book.

I would also like to thank Helen Baron, Malcolm Bray, Andrew Chapman, Trish Cross, John Dean, John Hacksman, Margaret Holbrough, Stuart Neath, Gary Pyke, Elaine Quigley, Barbara Reik, and David Thompson.

Introduction

This book takes the mystery out of the extensive range of tests that employers set for applicants as part of a recruitment and selection procedure, or as part of a development programme for current employees. It will be useful if you are at any stage in your career where you expect that you may have to face selection tests of any kind, in addition to producing a good written application and giving a good interview.

The book will familiarize you with the most commonly used types of tests and also help you to prepare more effectively for whatever you will face – whether it is sitting a battery of aptitude tests, giving a presentation, completing a personality questionnaire or solving a business or communication problem. However, the main focus here is on verbal reasoning tests, numerical reasoning tests, personality questionnaires and business exercises, because these are the most widely used forms of testing and operate across the greatest range of different jobs. This book will also help you understand why employers use these tests, what you can learn for yourself from your test results and how to reflect on your performance in a constructive way, so that you can do even better on future occasions.

In Part 1, there are hints and tips on how to prepare ahead intellectually, psychologically and practically for tests, information about what to expect, and how to ensure that your performance is as good as it can be on the day. Examples of the different kinds of questions and tests are given in each section. Part 2 of the book contains further test questions and exercises for you to work through, along with their answers so that you can check your results. Part 3 lists other sources of help and information that will be useful both to candidates and to employers who are considering using tests.

The word 'tests' is used in its broadest sense, not just to cover aptitude tests but to include personality questionnaires, management-style questionnaires, in-tray problems and presentation and discussion exercises.

Mention is also made of less common forms of testing such as graphology or handwriting analysis and the role that these currently play in recruitment and selection procedures. The book is aimed primarily at candidates who face tests, but employers, especially those who have not considered using various test procedures in the past, may also find it a useful guide.

Preparation is always valuable: you wouldn't take a driving test if it was the first time you had sat behind the wheel of a car, and none of us would expect to be flown from A to B by a pilot who had not passed all the appropriate tests. While your job may not be a matter of life or death, you – as well as your employers – will want to know that you have the right skills and qualities to do the job.

Finally, the emphasis of this book is that taking 'tests' is not necessarily a bad or unpleasant experience: with the right attitude you may even find that some of them are enjoyable and you may learn to learn from the test situations you encounter.

part one

brilliant selection test results

1 Testing times

In this chapter:

- Who is likely to face tests?

- When are you likely to be tested?

- Why do employers use selection tests?

Many of us enjoy testing our own mental agility or analyzing our own personality. We've all spent hours trying to complete a cryptic crossword or endlessly twiddling a Rubik's Cube that we've found lurking at the back of a cupboard or on a forgotten corner of a desk. And how many of us feel irritated when a self-assessment questionnaire in an old magazine in the dentist's waiting room has already been completed? Certainly, we are often drawn to completing questionnaires and quizzes that tell us more about our personalities if that knowledge is for ourselves. What we don't feel so comfortable with is being judged on our results by others.

If we are asked to complete a personality questionnaire as part of a selection process, we worry in a way that we wouldn't if we were showing off our qualities to a friend or colleague. We are happy to be first with a quick mathematical calculation if it's for our own benefit and entertainment, but we don't like knowing that we're being measured, assessed and rated on these abilities in order to forecast our likely success in a particular career. Even if education has been an enjoyable experience, most people are glad to leave behind the thought of tests and written examinations, but selection tests are something many of us will meet throughout our careers.

Who is likely to face tests?

Testing frequently forms part of the selection process for graduates seeking entry into various professions or large companies. Those who make mid-career moves upwards or even sideways to new companies or to obtain promotion within their current organization may also face a range of selection test hurdles on the way to their desired career goal. Many recruitment consultants and headhunters will employ a psychologist or be qualified themselves to set various aptitude and personality tests to candidates before they put them forward for consideration by particular employers.

Tests may be used to:

- select for jobs
- select for particular roles within an organization
- select for promotion
- select for staff development initiatives
- aid career choice.

Some careers will also have very specific entry tests that relate directly to the applicant's ability to perform the day-to-day tasks the job demands. If you want to be a fire fighter you have to pass certain physical tests, and you can't fly a plane if you are colour blind.

What this amounts to is that many of us will face selection tests other than interviews and applications on many occasions throughout our working lives – whether as school leavers, college and university graduates, business professionals, managers, technical staff and IT specialists and so on.

When are you likely to be tested?

At what stage in your career and at what stage in the recruitment process will you encounter tests? There are no absolute rules about this.

In some cases, after you have made a written application you may be asked to take a test or a batch of tests before you attend an interview. You may have an interview first and – if this is successful – be put forward to take tests.

If you are applying for graduate schemes with large organizations, you may be invited to a selection centre where tests of various kinds, plus individual and panel interviews, all take place over one or two days.

If you are applying for a job through a recruitment consultant, that consultant may put you through some tests either before or after you have been introduced to a likely employer.

At management development level, the structure of the process is likely to be far more like that at a graduate selection centre.

Why do employers use selection tests?

To verify applicants' claims

Selection tests provide a different kind of measure and different information about the candidate than that obtained from either written applications or interviews. With a written application – whether an application form or a CV and accompanying letter – the candidate may have spent a great deal of time ensuring that they put together the most appropriate and most positive information. Candidates might have sought quite legitimate help with this process – perhaps using the professional help of a careers consultant, a human resource expert, or an experienced friend. However, a recent survey has suggested that as many as 71 per cent of CVs contain dishonest information. This refers not to the legitimate attempt by any candidate to paint themselves in the best possible light, but to actual factual untruths. Apparently, altering a class of degree, inventing additional GCSEs or A levels, changing a job title and even inventing periods of employment, are more common than we are aware of. The financial services sector has certainly taken this on board: software is now being developed to find out whether applicants have poor financial histories, debt problems, etc., so that any suspicions about their character may be allayed.

Of course, aptitude tests will not measure a person's truthfulness, but they can help verify candidates' claims that they possess a whole range of relevant and desirable skills. Candidates may state quite truthfully that they have good verbal reasoning or numerical and calculating skills, but an aptitude test will actually prove this. It is not so much that employers suspect candidates of being deliberately dishonest – it's only a minority who will falsify information, invent examination results or create periods of employment that never existed. The concern is far more likely to be one of candidates understandably presenting only the most positive information, or of listing the skills they believe they are expected to have. What a test should do is show how much of these skills they really do have.

Many people – both candidates and recruiters – see interviews as the most significant part of a selection procedure. Yet interviews can be idiosyncratic and do not always act as an accurate predictor of how a candidate is going to perform in a specific role within a particular team. Some people are very good at being interviewed – there may well be managers reading this book who might feel they have recruited the wrong candidate in the post because they were misled by excellent interview skills.

It is estimated that biographical interviews are around 40 per cent accurate in predicting someone's likely success in a job. Biographical interviews broadly follow the areas covered on a CV or application form, for example someone's education and employment history, professional experience, outside interests, etc. In contrast, criteria-based interviews yield around a 70 per cent level of predictability. In these interviews the focus is on two or three of the most important personal qualities that will enable someone to perform in the role. For example, qualities such as leadership, teamwork, negotiating skill, organizational ability will be chosen and the candidate will be questioned very rigorously on when and how they have demonstrated these particular skills and asked to provide evidence, with concrete examples.

To sift out the best candidates from large numbers of applicants

A second reason why some employers may ask applicants to take a range of selection tests is because those employers are dealing with large numbers of applicants and they require some other measure than simply a written work record or academic history. This reason for testing may be quite common in the graduate job market. Large companies may be employing anything between ten and two hundred new graduate entrants, but they are likely to face at least ten times that number of applicants – often far more. The employer may want to use a method that is less labour intensive than hundreds of interviews, so tests are often used as an initial sifting mechanism.

In the UK the pool of available graduates has expanded greatly over the past two decades. Where previously a good degree was enough to make you stand out from the crowd, it is no longer such a distinctive measure. The batteries of tests that are applied offer some finer definitions that distinguish one candidate from another.

To cut out subjectivity

A further reason why testing may be used is that it cuts out the subjectivity that creeps into other selection methods – it prevents the subjective views of the selector having such a large impact. If a company is recruiting large numbers of people at the same time, for example a group of graduates or staff for a new project, it is under greater pressure to get that recruitment right. In a recruitment drive the employer wants as much certainty as possible that it will make appropriate choices.

To measure performance and aid career development

There has also been an increase in the numbers of employers who use a variety of aptitude tests, personality questionnaires and other exercises as ways of measuring performance and aiding career development for current employees, particularly middle and senior management. An organization may do this in the interests of efficiency, because it wants to be sure that it's using staff in the roles and functions for which they are most well qualified.

An organization may also offer these activities to help staff career development. Many organizations have found that offering good career development programmes increases staff retention rates – something of real importance if time and money are being invested in providing training, which will be wasted if staff then choose to take their skills elsewhere.

In addition, employers are facing a rapidly shifting market where attributes such as the ability to manage change and self-motivation to work from home are becoming increasingly important. Testing will help employers fit the right staff to the right positions.

To make the right choice

In short, recruiting the right staff is one of the most crucial issues for any employer. Businesses, schools, hospitals, local government departments and technical organizations all need the right people and ideally they need them to stay. All employers probably ask themselves three very basic but essential questions when they are recruiting staff:

- Can they do the job?
- Will they do the job?
- Will they fit in?

The types of 'test' described in this book are all designed to help human resource professionals, line managers and recruitment consultants answer these three important questions in the most accurate and objective ways available to them.

Top tips for success in tests

- Anticipate when you might be tested.

- Take all the steps on preparation outlined in Chapter 3.

- Try to see tests not as a threat but as an opportunity for you to demonstrate some of the qualities you have mentioned on your CV or at your interview in a 'real' situation.

- Remember that tests may benefit you as much as your employer – they can mean you get a job to which you are really well suited, gain a promotion or receive some further training that is really useful for your career development.

2   A testing world

In this chapter:

- Measuring mental processes

- Designing appropriate tests

- Different types of tests

- How tests are implemented

- Examples of the most common types of tests

- How tests are scored

Measuring mental processes

Some of us like the idea of gaining self-knowledge through a quiz in a magazine, or solving a problem in a puzzle book. But however much we may think that the results affirm what we are really like, such quizzes and problems are not in any way objective measures in the true sense of a psychometric test. This chapter gives a quick outline of psychometric testing without going into complex detail.

Philosophers, scientists and mystics have long been preoccupied with human nature, both its intellectual capacity and its ability to feel, to react, to relate and to behave in particular ways. But it wasn't until the birth of psychology and its expansion in the early part of the twentieth century that people really began to question what aspects of a person you could measure, how you might compare them with one another and how you might put this knowledge to use in education and in selecting those with the most appropriate skills and qualities to undertake particular tasks in the workplace.

The psychologist Donald Spearman was the first to formalize this idea with the development of the IQ in 1908. He observed that when testing people on three groups of abilities (ability with words, ability with numbers and ability with spatial concepts) there appeared to be a correlation between them. People who were good at one of these probably also did reasonably well at the other two. He therefore concluded that there was something that constituted general intelligence. This idea has probably fuelled one of the fiercest debates in psychology over past decades, but what is relevant here is that those three particular abilities are still the most frequently tested in selection and recruitment today.

Defining terms

At this point it is useful to include a brief glossary of everyday terms, which we tend to use fairly loosely. This is quite acceptable for normal conversation, but the terms need a little unpicking for a book like this.

Glossary of testing terms

Ability	The extent to which an individual demonstrates the capacity to use certain skills. Ability often refers to aptitude and attainment taken together, i.e. the level you have already reached and your potential to go further.
Aptitude	A person's ability to use certain skills and to have the potential to develop these in the future, for example someone may start to learn a foreign language and grasp the structure and the vocabulary quickly, but to begin with they will not have attained a high level of fluency, because the knowledge simply isn't there yet. An example of an aptitude test might be a test that

	assesses someone's ability to become a computer programmer, rather than measuring what facility they already have with information technology.
Attainment	The level that someone has already reached – they may have a GCSE in mathematics, so this is an attainment, and they may also have the aptitude to go further. A typical attainment test is the driving test or an oral test of fluency with language.
Competencies	Included in many job specifications, this refers to a group of skills and abilities, personality traits and experience which, taken together, are essential or desirable for a particular job. The terms 'essential' or 'desirable' are often used to categorise the competencies required, as outlined in any application information.
Intelligence	One overall measure of a person's range of abilities. Whether intelligence really is one facet that can be measured overall or whether it is made up of a whole range of separate abilities is fiercely debated by psychologists.
Skill	Used in a generic way, this can include being good at particular crafts or trades, or good with words or with technology. It denotes a level someone has already attained, rather than a potential.
Strength	Any of someone's perceived good points: for example an aptitude for dealing with numbers or a sensitivity in listening to other people.

It is unnecessary to get too obsessed with these definitions – when you are completing application forms or talking at a job interview you are hardly likely to be marked down on a slight semantic imperfection. But what you do need to know is that in the field of ability testing (rather than personality testing), aptitude and ability are the most usual words you are likely to encounter.

Designing appropriate tests

Until the 1970s the majority of careers guidance in the UK was based on checking what skills and aptitudes a person had and then matching them to the right place in the job market. This was the notion of personal choice and preference and finding a job that suited you. These days occupational psychologists and human resource staff undertake job analyses to find out just what is required to perform successfully in a particular role. They can then use tests to match a candidate's aptitudes and personality more closely to those required for the job.

Developing a test is a lengthy and complex procedure because a test has to fulfil three very important criteria. To be of any use, tests have to be objective, reliable and valid.

Objective

Tests must be objective so that they treat all test takers in the same way. Everyone has to be given the same amount of time, identical instructions and the marking and interpretation has to be fair. This becomes a little more complicated because factors like age, gender, ethnic background and educational experience may need to be taken into account, so that candidates are marked like against like. If you gave the same verbal reasoning test to a group of car mechanics, a group who had just graduated with honours degrees in modern languages, and a group of top level barristers, you would not expect the same scores and it would not be fair to score one group against the other.

Of course, tests are generally far more refined than this and will be designed to test a particular group of people at a particular occupational level. Psychologists will get this level right by putting groups of people through their tests during the tests' validation stage. They will then be able to work out what will be average, below average and above average results on the test. In this way, when a test is being marked, it can be checked against these norm tables and a more meaningful result will be produced.

Reliable

Tests have to be reliable in two ways. If one candidate takes similar tests a few weeks or a few months apart, the scores they achieve should not be wildly different, unless there has been some other influence, such as ill health or tiredness, or intensive practice taking place between the two tests. Tests also have to be reliable across groups of candidates. If an employer tests a group of candidates from a similar background, say graduates from different universities studying a range of subjects, and then tests a similar group of different applicants the following day, the test should sort the two groups in a consistent way.

Valid

Tests have to be valid – they have to test what they claim to be testing. For a test to be useful to employers it also has to measure those aptitudes and aspects of personality that really are relevant to the jobs being filled. Well-designed tests will be based on detailed job analyses that will look at the functions and competencies required within a job.

It is quite possible to design appropriate tests for any level and any type of job, so long as what is measured is an ability that is important to the job. There are tests available for all levels and types of job: call centre staff, administrative assistants, production line workers, designers, lawyers, accountants, company directors, etc. The more varied a range of abilities the job requires – especially in many graduate jobs and upwards – the more likely it is that core abilities rather than more narrow skills will be assessed.

With more than a thousand different tests available, they can be daunting for employers as well as candidates. Occupational psychologists employed by human resource departments and by test design companies look carefully at the work requirements for a particular job and can help employers to use tests appropriate to their needs. Although tests are available to work with any level of employee, the most common use of tests is for graduate level upwards.

Key points about tests

- Tests are designed to measure either your typical performance or your maximum performance.
- A good test must treat all candidates fairly.
- A test must test what it claims to test.
- A test must be consistent over time.

Different types of tests

Verbal tests

Verbal tests (covered in depth in the following chapter) range from simple spelling tests, tests of understanding of grammar and the meanings of words, through to verbal reasoning tests that ask you to deduce information from sometimes quite complex written material.

Clerical and data checking tests

These are exactly as they sound. You are presented with data which you have to check for accuracy. For example, you will be given two columns of names and addresses that look identical but which contain some minor differences. The task is to spot these differences. Speed and accuracy are being tested here.

Numerical tests

These range from simple arithmetic tests through to numerical reasoning tests that require you to interpret various forms of data. The tests can be quite complex and are covered in depth in the following chapter.

Diagrammatic or abstract reasoning tests

These are tests of your perceptual reasoning. Since they do not rely on an understanding of language (needed for many numerical reasoning tests, not just verbal assessments), these diagrammatic tests are believed to give a good measure of general intelligence.

Spatial reasoning tests

These tests measure the ability to visualize solid objects in two-dimensional forms and to manipulate shapes in two dimensions. They are different from diagrammatic reasoning, which is based on interpreting information or finding patterns through visual representations.

Mechanical reasoning tests

These tests are designed to assess your knowledge of mechanical processes – those processes that cause machinery to work, wheels to turn in certain directions, structures to hold together, etc. The tests are generally designed so that, in theory, those without a scientific background can achieve a high score. However, if you are the sort of person who takes an interest in how your car engine works, this will help.

Work sampling

Work sampling is exactly what it says. Instead of being given a test of certain abilities or undergoing a personality measure to see whether you fit the personality specification, you are given a sample of the work to do. This is now so common that we don't always worry about it as much as other forms of selection test. For example, if you are applying for an IT admin. job you might be asked to perform some typical tasks such as word-processing a document, entering some data or retrieving some data. For electrical work, you may be required to wire a circuit, while if you apply for a job in a restaurant you might be asked to carry several plates to see how you cope. It is really a matter of commonsense about what sort of preparation you can do and whether you will be given notice about these tests. You should be notified if you are going to do a test such as word-processing or electrical circuitry, but you would not expect to receive written notification that you will be asked to carry a stack of plates or make some sandwiches.

Physical tests

These are tests of strength or stamina. You are only likely to face such tests if you are applying for a job where physical strength is relevant, for example if you want to join the armed forces, the fire service or the police. If you are contemplating these careers you will know that physical fitness is one of the qualities on which you will be assessed and you will be given notification of these tests. If you think the tests are likely to be a problem, you should start your preparation well in advance and seek advice from a qualified fitness coach or instructor.

How tests are implemented

Will you encounter the same tests set by different employers?

It would be very surprising if you encountered identical tests in any two places, but you may encounter tests that look very similar to one another. A few large testing companies do provide tests for very large numbers of employers, but they will not give identical sets of questions to each employer. If you are a graduate applying to several large organizations, you are likely to find yourself taking similar groups of tests on different occasions, but you probably will not have seen the actual questions before. There are also some tests that look very different from the more typical graduate and management aptitude and ability tests.

How long do tests last?

Some tests, such as spelling, basic arithmetic and clerical checking, may last only 10 or 15 minutes. The more complex reasoning tests vary in length, but 25–40 minutes per test is not uncommon and you often take two or three of these tests in succession. A typical test session will last around two hours.

What kinds of organizations use tests?

Companies and organizations representing every field of employment will use tests – but this does not mean they all do. Areas where testing is prevalent include accountancy, management consultancy, IT, retailing, engineering, building services, financial management, human resources, marketing, advertising, project management, logistics, product development and customer support. Bodies such as the civil service, local government, armed services and the police all use testing as part of their selection process and many of these tests are designed specifically for the organization concerned.

Examples of the most common types of tests

There are far more than a thousand tests on the market, but those outlined below represent some of the more common types of test you are likely to encounter.

The GAP series

Saville and Holdsworth develop and publish an extensive range of tests, but those most likely to be encountered by new graduates are tests in their GAP (General Abilities Profile) series. These include verbal tests (comprehension), numerical tests (data interpretation) and diagrammatic reasoning (where you are asked to work through a series of diagrams by following arrows in order to interpret commands).

The ABLE series

Published by Oxford Psychologists Press, the ABLE series is different from many graduate aptitude tests because it is based on a series of what look like mini 'in-tray' type exercises. These focus on such specific business skills as business decision analysis, critical information analysis, financial appraisal and legal interpretation. The tests are designed in such a way that they do not require prior knowledge of a particular topic or of a specific business or commercial sector and if candidates work effectively they can learn as they proceed through the test and put that learning into practice. This test series is also described in Chapter 9 on equal opportunities.

The GMAT

The GMAT or Graduate Management Admissions Test is not a recruitment selection test as such, but is used to select applicants for graduate management programmes in the USA and for many Masters in Business Administration (MBA) programmes in Europe and the UK. Many of the questions that appear in the test are similar to those in selection aptitude tests. There is a verbal section, consisting of verbal comprehension, verbal reasoning and sentence completion questions; a quantitative test, which assesses your ability to interpret and analyze data; and, somewhat differently to most selection tests, an analytical writing section, which asks you to write two short essays on business, current affairs or social sciences topics. Details of access to some GMAT practice material are given in sources of information in Part 3 at the end of this book.

The Morrisby Profile

This is a test that is used in vocational guidance rather than recruitment and selection, so if you use the services of a careers consultant, this may well be one of the tests that you may take. The test assesses verbal, numerical, spatial, perceptual, mechanical and diagrammatic ability and includes a personality questionnaire and an occupational interest questionnaire. The report that is produced then generates some job suggestions, together with detailed information on all the ability tests and personality tests.

How tests are scored

Not all test scores are used in the same way. In some cases they may be used to choose the best from a group of applicants, for example the 10 per cent with the best scores will be successful in getting through to the next round of selection, being offered a job, etc. On other occasions selectors will have a target score in mind and anyone who achieves this level will be successful. If you are tested as an individual, rather than in a group selection exercise, then this second way of scoring is more likely to be used. You don't really pass or fail aptitude/ability tests; you either achieve or don't achieve the level that a particular employer is looking for.

3 Preparation counts

In this chapter:

- Intellectual preparation

- Verbal tests

- Numerical tests

- Diagrammatic reasoning tests

- Psychological preparation

- Commonsense preparation

Preparation is one of the four big Ps of test taking – preparation, practice, performance and positive thinking.

There are many steps you can take to ensure that you do perform at the optimum of your ability on the day you take the test. Preparation falls into three categories – intellectual preparation, psychological preparation and what we might choose to call commonsense or practical preparation.

Intellectual preparation

You should start your preparation well ahead of the day that you are going to sit the test.

Employers should, if they are following best practice, notify you in advance that you are going to have to take tests. You should not turn up expecting only an interview and then find that you are going to sit a battery of tests and selection exercises. Similarly, if you are going through a development procedure as part of your current post, connected with either career development, change of role or promotion opportunities, then your human resource department or the psychologists involved should give you detailed information about what to expect.

The suggestions that follow on preparation are most relevant to those who are applying for a job, especially at graduate recruitment level upwards.

The kind of tests you have to sit will affect your preparation. If you are simply told that you will have to sit a range of tests, then you might reasonably assume that it is most likely to include a group of ability tests and the most common combination of these is verbal reasoning, numerical reasoning and diagrammatic reasoning. To some extent the area of work you are applying for will dictate the tests you are most likely to encounter. Diagrammatic reasoning tests, for example, are used to select those who are most suitable to work in computing, especially software and systems development, whereas verbal reasoning tests are used across an extensive range of jobs in management, retail, leisure, customer services – in short, any job where you may be called upon to use your communication skills.

TEST TROUBLES

Some people worry that if tests are measuring fixed abilities, then preparation will make little difference to their overall score. Before jumping to this conclusion remember that:

> being familiar with what to expect will help

> the first time you take an aptitude test your score may be low because you are not used to doing them

➤ you may have been out of the tests and examination system for some time, so training yourself to do better will help

➤ you may be tested for abilities that you have not exercised for a long time, such as numerical ability, so practice can vastly improve your score.

So how different are these tests to other examination or testing procedures that you have experienced? Whatever the type of test, the answers are nearly always multiple choice, so if you have only recently left school you will be familiar with these. You will see a question and this will be followed by three or four possible answers and you have to choose the correct one. Some typical test paper questions are included in Part 2 of this book, where you will see the examples laid out in exactly the way they would be in many test papers. This chapter will show you some individual examples of different types of question and some particular ways of preparing for each kind of test.

Verbal tests

Verbal tests might be the ones that we anticipate giving us fewest problems. We speak and write all the time and verbal communication and usage is absolutely a part of everyone's everyday life. But even if we do not expect to have too hard a time with these tests, they can be daunting. This was brought home to me when working with university undergraduates and postgraduates who sometimes came to discuss their test results with me. Those who were studying predominantly word-based academic disciplines were always particularly surprised and upset if they had found a verbal test difficult, or if they found that they had not achieved a good score. Verbal tests, however, are not the same as actually using words, conversing, discussing, presenting or writing. They test very specific skills, as outlined below.

Spelling tests

Since you cannot be asked how to spell a word by having it written down, the tests will take various forms. For example, two spellings of the same word are given and you are asked to choose the one which is correct.

Example 3.1

accommodation

accomodation

In this instance the first spelling is correct and you will be asked to tick it, put a circle round it or underline the incorrect word.

Sometimes you will be given a whole list of words where some are spelt correctly and some incorrectly and you have to pick out those that are wrong.

Example 3.2

collaborate

discerning

advisery

assimilate

promolgate

controversy

developement

improvement

Three of the above words are spelt incorrectly and should be underlined

Answer

advisory

promulgate

development.

It is a myth that employers do not care about spelling any more just because everyone now uses spell-checkers. The spell-checker offers you several options if you have spelt the word wrongly, but if you don't know what you are aiming for you can still make a mistake. The spell-checker does not question the meaning of the words you have used. Fairly or unfairly, poor spelling is often equated with a generally sloppy or careless attitude and there may still be occasions when you are writing down something for a customer, a client or a colleague and do not have any recourse to electronic support.

Various spelling tests can be found in Part 2 of this book, and you will also find a list of words that are often misspelt on page 34.

Testing your understanding of word meanings

You may be given a group of four words and asked to pick out the word which has a different meaning from the other three.

Example 3.3

(a) weary   (b) tired   (c) exhausted   (d) fatigued

Answer

The odd one out is 'exhausted' because this has another meaning: a supply or a resource can be exhausted, so the word is not only a description of feeling as if you need a rest. It is easy to pick 'weary' because this is an adjective and all the others are past tenses of a verb.

Example 3.4

(a) quick   (b) fast   (c) rapid   (d) running

Answer

In this example, the odd one out is the word 'running' which is the only verb. Again, there is a slight trick in the question because both the words 'rapid' and 'running' tend to make you think of water and lead you in the wrong direction.

In these tests you will often find more than one answer that seems to be right, so you need to think carefully about the result and go through a logical and methodical process.

In another version of this type of question you are given a word and then asked to choose a word with a similar meaning from a given list of four or five words.

Example 3.5

Quarrelsome means the same as:

(a) furious (b) aggressive (c) argumentative (d) irritable

Answer

The correct answer is 'argumentative' because while all four words are associated with bad-tempered behaviour, only argumentative and quarrelsome mean liable to disagree and take a contrary point of view.

Sometimes you will be asked to find the opposite to a word by selecting from a given list.

Example 3.6

Fertile means the opposite of:

(a) desert (b) barren (c) arid (d) fecund

Answer

The correct answer is 'barren'.

There are also tests that ask you to work out the relationship of one word to another.

Example 3.7

Wardrobe is to clothes as dustbin is to:

(a) dirt (b) recycling centre (c) rubbish (d) waste bin

Answer

The correct answer is 'rubbish', because a dustbin contains rubbish in the way that a wardrobe contains clothes.

TEST TROUBLES

When you are dealing with any questions about word meanings and word relationships, pay really close attention to the question. Note phrases like 'the same as' or 'the opposite of', because it is very easy to get into a rhythm of thinking that a series of questions that look similar is asking the same thing, when in fact there is a variety of question types.

When you are taking tests like these, remember that there are certain standard ways in which words relate to one another:

- words that have the same meanings, e.g. prohibition and ban
- words with opposite meanings, e.g. lively and lethargic
- words that signify part to whole, e.g. letter to word
- word sequences, e.g. Tuesday, Wednesday, Thursday
- words from the same category, e.g. colours, numbers, capital cities
- strange words that have two meanings, e.g. to cleave together, or to cleave, meaning to separate.

Grammatical usage tests

You will encounter these tests for some clerical and administrative jobs, but occasionally at higher levels too if a significant part of your work will involve producing good written material, reports, publicity brochures, press releases, etc.

Example 3.8

Which of the following sentences is grammatically correct?

(a) You can find a copy of our company's latest annual report on our website.

(b) You can find a copy of our companies latest annual report on our website.

(c) You can find a copy of our companies' latest annual report on our website.

(d) You can find copies of our five subsidiary companies' annual reports on our website.

Answer

The correct answers are (a) and (d).

People often make mistakes with apostrophes, but there is nothing mysterious about them. If something belongs to only one person or one object, e.g. a company, then the apostrophe comes before the 's'. If something belongs to a group of objects, e.g. five companies, then the apostrophe comes after the 's'. Unpick this by asking yourself whether it is one or many things that is being described.

In terms of preparation for aptitude tests it is probably not worth going into great detail to relearn all the basic rules of English grammar. But it is worth reminding yourself about differences between verbs, words of action, nouns, objects and adjectives, and words of description, because these will help when you are tackling any word meaning exercises where you have to pick out similarities, differences and relationships.

Word placement tests

Yet another type of verbal test asks you to place words that either sound similar or have similar spellings in the correct place in pairs or groups of sentences.

Example 3.9

Look at the following two sentences and put the correct word (either 'there' or 'their') into the blank spaces:

It had always been … intention to develop a new range of fashion products.

It was now at least six months since … had been any significant development taking place.

Answer

'Their' should be placed in the first sentence and 'there' in the second.

Beware of tests like these: don't always assume that you have to use both words, but work out which has the appropriate meaning and place it carefully.

More examples of word placement tests can be found in Part 2.

Verbal comprehension tests

One of the most common features of verbal ability tests is a series of verbal comprehension tests. These give you a short passage to read through, followed by a few statements based on information contained in the passage. It is a short job to work out whether these pieces of information are true or false, using what you have read.

Example 3.10

'Very large portions of two European languages, English and Italian, have evolved from the same root – Latin. In a real sense English and Italian are like dialects of each other. The fact that they do not look alike at first sight is partly because English has changed substantially over time and partly because English has two roots – Indo-Germanic and Latin. The double origin accounts for the fact that English is a very rich language and there are very often two words in English that mean essentially the same thing.'

(a) Italian has only one root.	True/False
(b) English and Italian share their Latin roots.	True/False
(c) Italian is not a rich language.	True/False
(d) English has two roots.	True/False
(e) In English there are often two words that mean the same thing.	True/False

Answers

(a) False

(b) True

(c) False

(d) True

(e) True

The most important technique here is to base your answers on what is actually written down – this is not a test of your general knowledge or a point for debate. For example, you cannot draw the conclusion that 'Italian is not a very rich language' from what you have read – you have been given a reason why English is a rich language, but you have not been told that Italian is not rich. Always go back and ask yourself to answer any questions like these based only on the text that is there in front of you. You must not rely on any prior knowledge you have on the topic.

This type of test is extremely common, particularly in graduate selection tests. Further examples provided by Saville and Holdsworth are given in Part 2 of this book.

Top tips to improve your spelling and use of words

■ If you do not own a dictionary, buy one. Don't leave it unopened on your book-shelf – always look up any word of which you don't know the spelling and/or the meaning. (Colin Dexter, the creator of Inspector Morse, says that he never reads any book without having a dictionary by his side. In his case this has certainly paid off – the vocabulary he uses in his bestselling novels is apparently the largest of any writer.)

■ Buy a thesaurus – it will help you with word meanings and finding alternative words to use in your own writing.

■ Have a healthy suspicion of your spell-checker: it is fine if your spelling is approximately correct, but you need to know enough to know that you have got something wrong. Be aware of different company policies on UK or US spelling for words such as organise/organize, colour/color and programme/program.

■ If you are not normally a reader, try to read a little more. Choose something that interests you – quality newspapers, journals of interest in your academic or professional field and any fiction and non-fiction that you think you will enjoy.

■ Games like Scrabble can be useful, although this might develop your lateral thinking as much as your spelling – no prizes for spelling the word 'quiz', but it gets a tremendous Scrabble score.

■ Design some of the word meaning tests described above for yourself – working through the process in reverse is very useful.

■ Get a friend to do your word tests. If they have difficulty, then teach them the process you have already been through – explaining to someone how to do something is a great test of whether you really know how to do it yourself.

■ Be aware of some of the most common mistakes in spelling. For example, make sure that you know the correct usage of the word 'its' as in the posses-sive (its own, its recent or its previous) as opposed to 'it's' short for 'it is' ('it's easy to see', 'it's difficult to imagine', or 'it's not always the case').

TEST TROUBLES

There are some words that are frequently spelt wrongly. Those below are the ones you are most likely to meet in either a test or a business context:

advisory   analysis   affect   assessment   businesses   committee controversy   correspondence   development   discerning   effective efficient   forecast   fundamental   improvement   independent maintenance   persistent   separate   syndicate

Numerical tests

An ability to deal with numbers is a big requirement in so many businesses and professions. This does not mean that everyone has to be a top mathematician capable of dealing with complex formulae, algebra and trigonometry. It means an ability to interpret numbers for business purposes. It is likely that if you ask someone what jobs involve numbers their answer will be 'accountant', 'actuary' or 'bank manager', but anyone looking at profit and loss in a shop, a restaurant or an IT company, or anyone responsible for their own department's budget has to have a basic understanding of what numbers mean.

Basic arithmetic tests

Example 3.11

9 + 13

Answer

22

Additions are not normally as simple as this, though some arithmetic tests do start with simple questions and become gradually more difficult. Remember also that tests are timed and therefore with straightforward arithmetic you will be expected to cover a lot of ground in a short time.

Brush up on dealing with percentages. Statistical information forms a part of so many jobs and very often information is given as percentages.

Example 3.12

What is 13% of 127?

Answer

16.5

Example 3.13

If 59 = 25%, what equals 100%?

Answer

236

Problem-solving arithmetic questions

Example 3.14

Nineteen members of staff all wish to contribute to a retirement gift for the twentieth member of their department. They decide that they will all contribute a fixed amount, but this amount will be pro rata according to whether they work full-time or part-time.

Ten members of the department work full-time.
Four members of staff work three full days a week.
Five members of staff work for two and a half days a week.
The total amount collected is £149.00.

How much were those who worked for three days a week asked to contribute?

Answer

£6.00

Some questions include some basic algebra.

Example 3.15

If 3x + 3 = 15, what is x?

Answer

4

Example 3.16

If 4x − 4 = 20, what is x?

Answer

6

Data interpretation tests

Data interpretation tests form the basis of many numerical reasoning tests, since these present the sort of problems you will meet in a work situation.

Example 3.17

Look at the following table with its questions and answers.

Use of local leisure facilities

	Percentage of adults over 18 using local leisure facilities			
	Adults 1999	Adults 2001	Males 2001	Females 2001
Swimming	10.5	14.5	6	8.5
Squash courts	11	9	7	2
Yoga classes	21	25	7	18
Weights and circuit training	22	19	13	6
Exercise classes	12	16	6	10

Assume for the purposes of this exercise that everyone involved was taking part in only one activity.

(a) In which year were the greatest number of people taking part in some kind of exercise?

(b) Were a higher proportion of males or females taking part in leisure activities of some kind in 2001?

(c) What was the most popular activity overall over the two years in question?

(d) What percentage of men took part in leisure activities in 2001?

Answer

(a) 2001

(b) Females

(c) Yoga classes

(d) 39%

Preparing to take numerical tests

■ Don't be put off by minus numbers – they can still be correct.

■ Remember that a minus multiplied by a minus always equals a plus.

■ A minus multiplied by a plus always equals a minus.

■ Make yourself familiar with percentages – they occur frequently when you are interpreting statistics and they are not really difficult. Set yourself a few to work out and then check them with a calculator.

■ Work the problem in both directions with questions like: 'What is 17% of 347?' and 'If 43% = 72, what is 100?'

■ Don't be put off by decimals or by adding or subtracting numbers with decimal points.

■ Don't be put off by fractions.

■ Remember, percentages, decimals and fractions all represent ways of breaking something into parts and are simply ways of quantifying proportions.

Remind yourself of very basic statistical concepts – mean, median and mode:

■ mean is the calculated average

■ median is the midpoint

■ mode is the most common.

Example 3.18

If temperatures in the Mediterranean for ten days in May were as follows, what was the median temperature?

Day 1   14C

Day 2   17C

Day 3	16C
Day 4	15C
Day 5	18C
Day 6	20C
Day 7	19C
Day 8	21C
Day 9	21C
Day 10	22C

Answer

The median is 18C because it occurs halfway between the lowest and the highest points (14C and 22).

Familiarize yourself with patterns of numbers:

■ basic tables, e.g. 2, 4, 6, 8, 3, 6, 9, 12, etc.

■ squared numbers, e.g. 2, 4, 16, 64, 5, 25, 125, 625, etc.

■ square roots, e.g. square root of 9 is 3, of 36 is 6, etc.

■ prime numbers (numbers only divisible by 1 or by themselves), e.g. 7, 11, 13, 17, etc.

Although you will not necessarily be tested on all of these, some forms of test ask you to look for patterns in groups of numbers, so reminding yourself of these gets you more used to number patterns.

Look at graphs and tables in text books, trade journals and the financial press. This information is usually given with a written explanation – and it may be exactly this kind of written explanation that you are asked to provide when presented with a graph or a chart as part of a numerical reasoning test.

Remind yourself what different charts look like in Figures 3.1, 3.2 and 3.3.

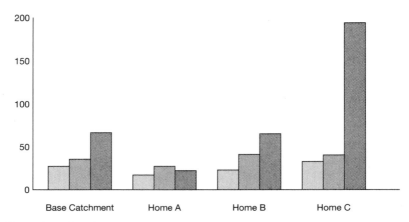

Figure 3.1 Bar chart

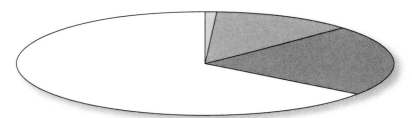

Figure 3.2 Pie chart

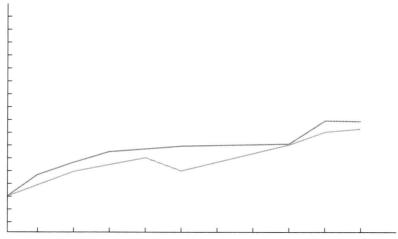

Figure 3.3 Graph

Top tips for taking numerical tests

- Make sure you are familiar with the functions of a calculator – you are often allowed to and required to use one in test sessions.

- Do calculations in your head that you would usually do on a calculator. You could add up your shopping bill as you go round a supermarket, or add up what you have spent if you order something from a mail order catalogue. You can always double-check the figures with a calculator afterwards to be sure you got the answer right and to remind yourself of the process.

- Make up problems of your own.

- Look at the financial and business press, which gives plenty of examples of financial data.

- Look at company annual reports.

- Do conversions of pounds sterling or euros into other currencies in your head.

- Explain basic mathematical processes to friends who are very good with numbers.

- Don't be afraid of numbers.

Diagrammatic reasoning tests

Finding patterns

Some tests ask you to find patterns or make links between different sets of information such as letters and numbers.

Example 3.19

What comes after A, B, D, G?

Answer

K: because A and B are one letter apart, B and D two letters apart, etc.

Example 3.20

If coffee is 3, 15, 6, 6, 5, 5, what is tea?

Answer

20, 5, 1: because numbers have been used to represent their respective places in the alphabet.

Example 3.21

What comes after red, blue, green?

(a) turquoise   (b) pink   (c) yellow   (d) brown

Answer

Yellow: because the three previous colours have each lengthened by one letter.

This is an example where you can get thrown off the scent as you try to recall the order of the spectrum or look for something far more complicated than the straightforward logic required.

Diagrammatic reasoning

These tests are popular with employers for two reasons. First, they do not rely on use of particular language skills for a successful performance, and second, they appear to be good predictors of success in working in such fields as computer programming. The tests provide a good measure of general intellectual reasoning because you are asked to find the underlying logical processes and solutions to a problem.

Example 3.22

Look at this diagram and decide how the sequence should continue.

   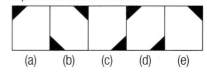

(a)   (b)   (c)   (d)   (e)

Answer

The correct answer is (b) because its diagonally opposite pair follows each single triangle. If you moved the single triangle one to the right, the only blank space would be the corner, which is diagonally opposite to it. These are the sorts of patterns that you have to seek out in diagrammatic tests.

Top tips for taking diagrammatic reasoning tests

- Separate out the different elements that can be altered in these diagrams: shapes, orientation of shapes, number of lines or other elements involved, different colours, shaded or white areas. Once you start to identify these, the diagrams look far less daunting.

- Some magazine quiz books and even newspapers offer examples of these abstract brain teasers, so make use of them.

- When you have learned to solve these tests, explain them to someone who hasn't.

- If your work and studies have not asked you to work in this abstract way, these questions can look frightening: don't let them put you off.

Psychological preparation

Relaxation

Feeling relaxed and confident about taking any sort of test is a very useful way to improve performance. Much of this relaxation and confidence comes directly from doing the intellectual preparation mentioned above. It is far easier to feel confident if you know you are well prepared for the sorts of tasks you might face.

Just as with any other situations in life, not all candidates will feel equally worried about taking selection tests. I have talked to some people, both undergraduates and more experienced professional and managerial staff, who really do enjoy going through some of these 'tests' and who prefer them to interviews. If, however, you are not in this group – and large numbers of people certainly are not – then being able to keep calm in potentially anxious situations is useful.

There are all sorts of relaxation tapes and advice guides on the market. Whether you want to use a product like this is very much a matter of personal choice, but some people do find that being talked through a relaxation exercise is beneficial. Try also some of the deep breathing exercises outlined in Chapter 8 on giving presentations and joining in discussions. These are designed to help you sound confident and project your voice more effectively, but they have an added benefit of steadying your whole body.

Another good relaxation exercise is to lie on the floor, on a mat or a carpet, and progressively tense and relax different parts of your body. Begin with your toes, scrunching them up as tightly as you can, and then gradually move up your feet, legs, etc., finishing with the muscle groups in your neck and face.

Some people already have a chosen exercise regime that helps – this may be yoga, Pilates or going to the gym or training for a marathon. It really doesn't matter what you choose – so long as it suits you.

Imagine the situation

Many hypnotherapists and counsellors dealing with stress management also teach their clients to visualize situations with positive outcomes. There is nothing strange or mysterious about this – it is a very common technique to help you feel more positive about coping with any situation, whether it is sitting a written test, giving a presentation or attending an interview.

Picture yourself turning up for the test, feeling calm and confident – arriving in good time, but not with so much time to spare that you have time on your hands. Picture the test room with its desks and chairs and decide whether you would like to sit near the front, at the end of a row, or close to a window if there is one. You are one of the first, though not the first, to arrive, so you can choose the spot that suits you best. Picture yourself feeling comfortable, breathing deeply and feeling quite eager to get started.

Follow this process through in your mind, making sure to picture the questions being not too difficult, your time management being good and you coming out at the end of the test session feeling that you have put in a good performance – at least the best you possibly could.

Although imagining that the questions are easy will not actually make them easy, having a positive and confident attitude will help. Sportsmen and women, musicians and actors will often apply techniques like this to aid their performances.

Banish negative thoughts

It is easy to impede your chances of success by allowing negative thoughts to crowd out positive ones. Things like 'I never do well at tests', 'I was hopeless at maths when I was at school', 'my memory isn't what it was', 'I hate doing things in timed situations', 'it's a long time since I have had to take any sort of test, I'll probably make a mess of it', all hinder good performance. If you feel that any of these really are true, e.g. 'I was never any good at maths at school', then make sure this is an area where you put in some extra preparation well before the test.

Commonsense preparation

If you are going for an interview with a company, or even if you are applying to it on spec, you try to find out as much about it as you can beforehand. This process is exactly the same for tests – the more you know about them, the more you know what they are likely to need.

- Make sure that you know when and where to turn up and that you have read all the instructions.

- Often, the employer will send you some practice material with answers, so that you can familiarize yourself with what the questions will look like. Use this wisely – if you cannot immediately get the answers right, read any advice given with the practice material and try to work out the process to achieve the right answer. Be just as scrupulous if you do get answers right – unpick the steps you went through to achieve this, so that you can use the same mental process on other similar questions in the real test.

■ If the tests are part of a graduate selection centre or a management development centre, the whole process could involve social events too, so ensure that you have the appropriate clothes with you.

■ If you have a disability or some other special concern about the tests, contact the employer or the testing organization as soon as you are invited to a test. There may be special arrangements that they can and should make on your behalf, but they will not be able to do this without due warning. Look at the equal opportunities section at the end of Chapter 9 and the sources of information in Part 3 of this book.

Top tips for preparation

■ Find out as much as you can about what sorts of test you will be taking.

■ Read the job description or any other information you have about the company – this will sometimes give you clues about what to expect. For example, if good numerical skills are stated as being essential, it might be reasonable to assume that these will be tested; if good presentation skills are important, you might be asked to give a presentation, etc.

■ Look at books that help you prepare for specific tests. For example, there are books on specific areas like computer aptitudes and there are books with extensive examples of diagrammatic tests.

■ Visit testing companies' and employers' websites.

■ Seek appropriate coaching if you think you need it.

You may also find it useful to complete the skills questionnaire, which will give you an idea of where you already have strengths/skills/knowledge and so help you refine your preparation. Even before you add up your scores for each of the six sections, you will easily see where your strengths – and therefore your weaknesses

– lie. In terms of aptitude tests, section 3 communicating relates to verbal reasoning, 6 numerical relates to numerical reasoning and 4 problem solving relates most closely to diagrammatic reasoning. Although the questionnaire is not an objective measure, it may help you clarify your likely areas of difficulty in test sessions.

Skills questionnaire

Rate how good you are at the following	Score 6 = high 1 = low
1 *Creative*	
Drawing, painting	
Performing music	
Writing creatively	
Using your imagination in work situations	
Being sensitive to aesthetic qualities	
2 *Influencing*	
Negotiating a deal or a successful outcome	
Persuading people around to your point of view	
Selling a product, a service or an idea	
Managing other people	
Organizing events, seminars, conferences, etc.	
Promoting ideas effectively	
3 *Communicating*	
Writing reports, summaries, proposals and letters	
Learning foreign languages	
Reporting on events	
Speaking in public	

▶ Understanding complex written information

4 Problem solving

Analyzing information

Using maps and other diagrammatic information

Restoring equipment

Detecting faults in a system

Following detailed instructions

5 Social

Relating to a wide range of people

Showing insight and understanding

Explaining, teaching, training

Offering support and advice

Listening to others

Building relationships and networks

6 Numerical

Interpreting graphs

Interpreting statistical data

Solving quantitative problems

Producing accounts and budgets

Interpreting financial information

4　The big day

In this chapter:

■ Before the test

■ During the test

■ After the test

If much of what follows seems obvious, then be patient – it is surprising how many people jeopardize and lower their test scores by making simple errors. This is because it is easy to make errors when you feel under pressure and are trying to concentrate very hard.

Before the test

Take care of yourself

This chapter is mainly about the day you take the test, but it is worth giving a little thought to the day, or at least the evening, before. Too much alcohol or caffeine before facing any mentally taxing task is not a good idea, so try to think carefully about what you eat and drink on the evening prior to a test. Try to get a good night's sleep, too – don't stay up into the small hours working through mental arithmetic problems, reading the financial press or testing your knowledge of words.

On the day of your tests, eat breakfast. Many people skip breakfast if they are busy or anxious, but it is not sensible to let your blood sugar plummet. You haven't eaten during all your hours of sleep, so give your system a bit of a boost. You will know which foods make you feel good and which make you feel lethargic. If your tests are at a graduate selection centre or a management development centre, then your food is likely to be taken care of, so make sure you take full advantage of snacks and mealtimes whenever they are offered.

Check instructions

You should have done this before the day itself, but make sure that you have read any instructions carefully. Ensure that you know:

- what time to turn up
- where to turn up
- who you should report to
- what you should bring with you
- a contact number and name in case any problems arise.

Turn up for the test

This sounds too obvious to be true, but significant numbers of people do not turn up for test sessions to which they have been invited – so just being there increases your chances of being successful.

With the increasing impact of technology you may find that some organizations ask you to do an initial test via a remote computer from home or at a careers centre. This would only be the case for an initial selection test, then, if you are successful at this stage, you would be invited to the more formal test sessions described here.

Turn up on time

This is true for any selection activity or appointment, but it is essential for test sessions. Plan your journey and, if you are driving, ensure that there will be somewhere convenient for you to park. These tests are run under the same sorts of conditions as you would encounter in any formal examination, so if you are late you will not be able to sit the tests at all. In most instances you will not be offered an alternative date. This may be a little different if you are taking some tests set by an individual recruitment consultant or occupational psychologist on your own, but if you are taking part in any group test this rule is pretty inflexible.

If something happens that really prevents you from turning up on time, it is worth letting the organization know, despite what has been said above. There may be a chance that you can be fitted in with another group of candidates and you have nothing to lose by asking – but you must have a very good reason.

Dress smartly

On many occasions you will be taking tests as part of a wider recruitment process, perhaps involving interviews, discussions and role-plays. Even if this is not the case, it is much better to be as smartly dressed as you would be for an interview – the other candidates probably will be and you don't want to stand out as the person who didn't bother. You do need to be comfortable though – this is not the day to squeeze into the trousers that will only just do up or try out a new pair of shoes that might cause you discomfort.

Time your arrival

Arrive with a little time to spare, but if you are very early take a walk or go and have a cup of tea. Think about things other than the tests – these are not the sort of examinations where you should be going over information in your head at the last minute.

If you are early, you may get a chance to pick a seat that you like – near a window, a door, at the back, or whatever you prefer. Companies normally ensure that their test conditions are pretty comfortable, so you won't have to fight for a desk or contend with demolition work going on in the room next door.

Check materials

The test instructions that you were sent in advance will have told you whether you will be working with pen/pencil and paper or whether – and this is increasingly the case – you will be working via a computer keyboard or a small hand-held computer. These factors themselves make no difference, but it is easier for you if you know what to expect. In most instances all the test materials will be provided, so you don't have to bring your own pencils, calculators or anything else, but you may want to have note paper to hand to work things out before you commit your answers to the test paper itself.

The materials will either be a question book with appropriate spaces for you to fill in your answers, a test booklet and a computer to key in your answers, or a computer screen displaying the questions and showing you where and how to fill in your answers. If the test does come in pencil and paper form, it is most likely to be a test booklet with questions set out so that you either fill in answers in sections after each question, or you are given a separate answer sheet to complete as you work through the questions. Have a look at the Saville and Holdsworth tests in Part 2 of this book to give yourself an idea of how the test questions are worded and what the answer format looks like.

If you wear glasses or use a hearing aid remember to take these items with you. Chapter 9 covers equal opportunities issues and gives you a little more information about what to do if you have a disability of any kind.

During the test
Comply with instructions

You will be told not to open your question book or work on your screen until the test administrator tells you to do so. Listen carefully to any other instructions they give, such as what to do if you have a problem, reminders about where to enter your name, candidate number, etc.

Read any instructions carefully. You will find clear information about how to fill in your answers, for example, putting a tick or a cross in a box, filling in a box, circling, underlining a letter or a number. These instructions will also tell you what to do if you realize you have answered something incorrectly and want to alter your answer. If you are doing a test via a computer, follow any instructions given carefully.

Don't be tempted to race ahead and start reading questions until you know what to do. This will waste precious time, as you may have to back-track. Some tests get progressively more difficult as you work through, so if you start looking at some of the questions you can make yourself panic unnecessarily and lose concentration on those questions you can answer perfectly well.

Use sample questions to your advantage

Very often there are some sample questions at the beginning of the test, which the administrator will work through with the whole group. You are given an opportunity here to speak up if there is anything you don't understand – do take advantage of this. There is no mileage in impressing other candidates by appearing to know everything – they aren't employing you. You need to be as sure as you can that you really do understand what is required of you.

Read questions carefully

The fact that you are working quickly does not mean you should skim-read questions. The essence of doing well on a verbal comprehension test is to read with care. With numerical tests, too, failing to read the question carefully can easily result in you choosing the wrong answer.

Use time wisely

In general, tests such as spelling, arithmetic and data checking are run over a shorter time (10–15 minutes) and you are unlikely to have time to double-check any answers – testing your speed and accuracy is built into the test. Verbal, numerical and diagrammatic reasoning tests are usually run over a longer period (anything from 20 to 40 minutes) and contain a smaller number of more complex problems that require a different strategy from you.

If there is something you cannot answer, move on to the next question – you can always come back later. If you do end up tackling questions out of sequence, take great care not to get out of sequence with your answers – this can happen so easily, with serious consequences for your test score.

TEST TROUBLES

You don't want to waste too much time chopping and changing from question to question if there are several that you find difficult. However, with diagrammatic tests it can sometimes help to move on to another question if you are really stuck – you may see things differently when you have worked through some other problems.

Continue to keep an eye on the clock – it is very easy to get engrossed in a particular question and lose track of time. Many candidates will not get right through all the questions, but the more correct answers you have the better, so move on rather than agonizing over a particular question.

Seek help

Once the test has started, the administrator will not be able to give you any help with questions that you do not understand (the only opportunity for that was when examples were worked through at the beginning). If this seems harsh, remember that it is exactly the same in any other examination situation, whether it is your GCSEs, your accountancy exams or your driving test.

TEST TROUBLES

If you have any problems during the test session other than finding the questions difficult, for example, you are having trouble with your computer screen, there seems to be something missing from your booklet or you feel unwell, then do attract the attention of the administrator – don't waste time trying to correct a technical problem yourself.

You can, however, ask for help if you have a problem such as your calculator won't work, your pencil breaks, something appears to be wrong with your test booklet or you feel unwell, i.e. anything personal or to do with the administration of the test rather than the questions and answers.

Work with intelligence

Studies have yielded different results on whether you should always go with your first answer. There is a tendency to believe that your intuition will have led you to the right answer first. There is no evidence for this; sometimes looking at something more carefully gives a better result. But don't take this approach to the extreme. Albert Einstein said that he often had to think through 99 different solutions to a problem and only the one-hundredth would be right – although you can stop short of this sort of intellectual rigour.

Don't just 'have a go' at answers unless you know this won't make things worse. Some tests are negatively scored, which means that as well as getting points for correct answers, you get points deducted for incorrect ones. Sometimes the administrator tells you about this, but sometimes the test booklet may just warn you not to guess answers. However, it is important not to let this approach stop you answering anything – since you won't have time to double-check everything, in some instances you will still not be sure if your answer is right, but you certainly won't score anything for handing back a blank answer sheet.

If you are going to guess some of your answers, still try to work out what may be right – if there are several options, eliminate those which you are sure are incorrect, so reducing the amount of guessing you have to do.

This applies especially to numerical tests because the majority of them are designed so that you don't have to carry out detailed and lengthy calculations, but just have to spot a correct answer. For example, if you are asked to multiply 17.5 by 11.3, the correct answer is 197.75. Answers you are offered could include 1977, 519 and 75, as well as the correct answer. You need to be able to estimate quickly that 17 times 11 comes to something between 160 and 200 and not something as small as just under 20 or as large as nearly 2000.

Look out for false trails

Similar looking numbers, similar sounding or looking words and distractions in the question can all catch you out. Say you are given a series of numbers: 7, 14, 21, 28. You might assume that the answer to an anticipated question is 35, but the question might ask what is the sixth number in this sequence, the answer being 42. You might barely glance at the question because your brain has already seen the pattern and gone forging ahead. Look out for phrases like 'the next but one' or 'what letter comes before the list shown'. Tests do not contain trick questions, but they do demand that you stay on your toes and remain alert to exactly what is being asked.

Don't be distracted

Don't fall into the trap of convincing yourself that the candidate at the next desk is doing better than you because they seem to have worked further through the test booklet. You don't know anything about the quality of their answers, so just concentrate on your own performance. Don't worry about pausing from time to time to collect your thoughts, or to give your shoulders a stretch and take a few deep breaths – just don't make it a long pause.

The last few minutes

You may be warned a few minutes before the test time is up. If you are, make use of this to return to any questions you now feel you can answer, or to squeeze in a few more questions before the time is up – answering a few more questions can make a significant difference to your score.

Keep calm – stay confident

Even though examinations or tests of other kinds are familiar to you, some test material looks very strange. Don't be daunted if you haven't done questions quite like this before. Don't discourage yourself by believing you have got things wrong – just work steadily on through the questions.

Keeping a sense of balance is important. Just reading the advice above may have confused you – you may feel that you are being asked to work quickly yet to spend time working things out, to watch the clock yet to work steadily. The advice is not really conflicting – it is all aimed at having a calm, orderly and sensible approach to dealing with tests.

Self-confidence is not going to transform you instantly into a superb mathematician or a brilliant wordsmith, but it does help – if you feel confident and positive you are far less likely to be put off. Tests can even be enjoyable – think of them as a mental exercise and the chance to do something different.

After the test

Your results

If you have taken a batch of aptitude tests – perhaps a verbal test, a numerical test and a diagrammatic test – as part of a graduate selection programme, and you are unsuccessful, it is not usual practice to give you your results. There is, however, no reason why you should not ask for these, though you are only likely to be given them over the telephone and not in a detailed feedback session. This can be frustrating and disappointing, but the alternative would be immensely costly to employers.

The employer may have various objectives in mind when setting the test, which you will not know. For example, knowing that you got 50 questions right out of 60 would be of no significance unless you also know that most other people got more than 55, or less than 45. Without knowing what the target score is, simply being given your results is meaningless. It is also often the case, particularly with graduate recruiters, that they may have different scores in mind according to the different jobs in which you are going to be placed. For example, the diagrammatic reasoning score may be very important for someone who is going into IT development, the numerical test score may be the most significant for those going into financial management, and verbal reasoning may be of most significance for those going into human resource management or marketing. The employer may be working to a whole set of different targets aligned to these job functions.

You may be more likely to be given back your results if your tests have been set as part of a development centre programme for middle and senior managers within a company, or if you have been tested individually by a recruitment or careers consultant, who is qualified to administer tests and to feed back their results.

As part of good test practice you should be informed about how your results will be dealt with at the beginning of the test session, so you should know whether there is a possibility of getting any feedback, in what form this feedback will be and, if you are not going to find out the results, what is going to happen to them.

Even if the test material looked unusual to you, if you compare it to other problems you have solved or assignments you have completed, you will probably have some basic sense of how you have done. You will know, for example, that you found numerical reasoning easier than diagrammatic, or that you found verbal reasoning easier than the other two tests.

This sense of how you think you have done will help you to decide how to prepare for future tests.

There are circumstances that will adversely affect your test score. If you are feeling unwell for any reason or are short of sleep or have other things preying on your mind, it is quite likely that you will get a lower score than you would if you were at your best. There may be nothing you can do about this – you probably won't be able to organize an alternative test date – but it does mean that you shouldn't read too much into that one result. So if you don't pass, or you don't get through to the next round of the selection, don't assume your performance will be exactly the same on future occasions.

Top tips for test taking

- Learn what you can about the tests before you take them.
- Be well rested and make sure you have had something to eat and drink.
- Be on time.
- Pay close attention to detail.
- Watch the clock.
- Be confident.
- Be positive.
- Reflect on your performance.
- Practise if you can.
- If you don't succeed, look on the test as good practice for the next time.

5 So much personality

In this chapter:

- Are you right for us?

- Personality questionnaires

- Examples of the most common types of personality tests

- Emotional intelligence

- How well do you know yourself?

Are you right for us?

Remember the three questions at the back of every employer's mind when recruiting staff:

- can they do the job?
- will they do the job?
- will they fit in?

Personality has a significant role to play in providing answers to all three questions and especially the second and third questions. Consider most working situations and remind yourself how the personality of your colleagues – those you manage and those who manage you – affects the day-to-day success of a business. If teams don't work well together or if a manager cannot motivate their staff, then productivity, sales targets, quality of service and customer care are all bound to suffer, along with staff turnover. This is something that employers really do want to get right.

Many notions about how management and organizations can work effectively have changed. At one end of the spectrum there are still companies which believe that the most effective tool of management is fear. At the other end are organizations encouraging all their staff to 'have fun' and indulge in mutual hugging sessions. Most employers – no doubt to the relief of those of us who have to work for them – don't opt for extremes like this, but do acknowledge that you will probably get the best out of people if they are reasonably happy, motivated and in a position to use their skills and talents to greatest effect.

Many employers like to use personality testing because they think the results are valuable – not just for the current job a candidate is applying for, but also for future situations. An applicant may be asked to take particular aptitude tests because they are being selected for IT development or for accounting work. But if they stay with the organization and progress successfully, they will move towards management roles where the characteristics measured by personality assessments become more significant than more specific and narrow aptitudes.

This is not a modern idea. Over a thousand years ago the Roman statesman Cicero tried to develop a formula for analyzing people's temperaments so that they might more effectively take on appropriate roles in society. Similarly, the Greek philosopher Plato was writing circa 400 years BC that the personality was made up of reason, spirit (which we might define as energy or enthusiasm) and appetite (which we might read as desire). He suggested that reason and spirit could be used to control appetite and in that way people could control their behaviour and develop the good in themselves. Terms that are still used in our everyday language – choleric, phlegmatic, melancholic and sanguine – are the four temperaments that were used to classify individuals in ancient Greece. Human nature has long had this tendency to seek ways to describe itself.

However, the twentieth century was the time when explanations and theories of the basis of personality really abounded, and psychoanalysis, behaviourism and later cognitive psychology jostled for supremacy. The discipline of psychology grew rapidly and led to many attempts to work out exactly what personality is and whether and how it can be measured.

Personality questionnaires

The principle behind the psychometric testing of personality is that it is possible to quantify implicit characteristics of people through self-reports of their feelings, thoughts and behaviour. To develop personality measures, large numbers of subjects are presented with statements describing various ways of acting or feeling. For example, 'I don't feel very confident when I meet new people' might be a statement that someone might make as a measure of self-confidence.

The data from large numbers of self-report questionnaires, peer assessments and observations of behaviour are used to ascertain the distribution of a trait within the general population. For example, some people might be very sensitive, others quite sensitive, others not very sensitive and some not sensitive at all, along a dimension or trait called 'sensitivity'. Once this 'sensitivity' scale has been developed it is possible to measure other individuals to see where they fall along this scale.

The arguments about whether people are born with these traits, whether they arise through learning or whether they are a result of the interaction between the two may be interesting, but they are not relevant to the test taker. What is relevant is that ways have emerged of measuring various traits, which appear to be quite accurate in predicting the behaviour and reactions of an individual. These predictions must also hold true over time – they would be of no use if someone completed a personality questionnaire on a Monday that suggested that they were very introverted, then the same test yielded a completely different result for that same individual two weeks later.

Despite some differences of opinion and some slightly different applications of the statistical methodology behind trait psychology, a reasonably consistent picture of the most significant traits has emerged. There appears to be consensus on five major traits, often referred to as 'the big five'. To confuse matters, the labels to describe these traits vary, but common terminology is:

- extroversion, assertiveness or impulse expression
- agreeableness, warmth, or docility
- conscientiousness or will to achieve
- emotionality or neuroticism
- intellect or openness to experience.

In some ways, these look a little strange because in everyday language all of these words already have either negative or positive associations. Many of us are happy to be described as agreeable, but would feel less comfortable with being described as docile. However, none of the traits is positive or negative, they are simply characteristics that each individual will exhibit to different extents. Many of the personality questionnaires in use today are based on a trait model of personality, measuring a variety of factors that are grouped around certain traits. However many factors are measured, they are likely to relate back to the five major traits.

Type theories are those that define an individual as being of a particular type. For example, a Freudian approach to personality classifies people according to where they get stuck as they pass through various phases of infant development. Of more relevance to occupational psychologists is the approach of Carl Jung who classified people as extroverted or introverted. One of the most widely used personality tools in management and staff development is the Myers-Briggs Type Indicator which has been developed around Jungian theory and which is outlined in a little more detail later in this chapter.

Your personality profile is of no use or interest to employers unless they have some way of knowing how that profile compares to the requirements of performing well in a particular role. Therefore, before personality questionnaires are used to select for particular jobs, results of similar questionnaires have to be produced for the population as a whole, or different groups within it, and also for those who are already working highly successfully in the jobs for which selection is being made. In this way, your profile can not just be measured against the

other candidates on the day – which would tell employers nothing –
but compared to the 'ideal' profiles for those jobs. One employer may
have several different 'good' profiles, for example if they are recruiting
for technical, managerial, financial and marketing positions.

Typical questions in personality questionnaires

Here are some examples of the types of question presented in personality questionnaires.

Example 5.1

I always enjoy meeting new people.

(a) True   (b) False

All you have to do is to tick or underline or cross out the appropriate
response. The test booklet will make it clear, but you only have the two
choices.

Other questionnaires will give you a 'third way':

Example 5.2

I am always methodical and organized when meeting a deadline.

(a) True   (b) False   (c) Can't say

Others will give you a set of statements and you are asked to choose
the one that best describes you:

Example 5.3

If I go to a party I …

(a) Get into the spirit of things quickly and am often the centre of attention.

(b) Tend to look for any familiar faces first and start talking to someone I know.

(c) Stand in a quiet corner and observe things for a while.

(d) Approach someone who looks shy and start talking to them.

You may be asked to rate a statement according to whether you agree or disagree.

Example 5.4

Other people always find it easy to talk to me.

Strongly agree	Agree	Unsure	Disagree	Strongly disagree
1	2	3	4	5

Many candidates feel more comfortable with tests like this because they prefer the degree of definition they feel it gives them.

Similarly you may be given descriptive words that you have to rate for agreement or disagreement. In this instance there would be instructions at the start of the test asking you to rate how strongly these words describe you.

Example 5.5

Calm

Lively

Conforming

Strongly agree	Agree	Unsure	Disagree	Strongly disagree
1	2	3	4	5

Preparing for and taking personality tests

Unlike aptitude and ability tests, there is not a great deal of preparation that you can do or need to do if you are asked to complete a personality questionnaire. However, they are still a method of selection about which many candidates feel very anxious. People tend to worry about what exactly is being tested and what might be revealed. Some people still feel as though someone is prying into their business in a slightly underhand way. Of course, personality questionnaires are not that sinister – you are asked about all sorts of aspects of yourself during a selection interview and the reports that your referees complete may ask your referees questions about your work style, the way you relate to colleagues, customers, etc.

You should always be informed that you are going to take a personality test and you should be told what will happen to the results and whether you are able to obtain any feedback. The 'test' session itself may be run in just as formal a setting as would be the case for any aptitude test, but the biggest difference is that there is unlikely to be a strict time limit. You will usually be given a recommended time – depending on the test concerned, this will be anything from 20 to 45 minutes, but you will not be penalized if you have not finished within this time and will normally be allowed to continue and complete the test. As with aptitude tests, you may be working with a booklet and answer sheet, a test booklet and computer, or increasingly you will complete the whole questionnaire via a computer.

With a personality questionnaire – unlike aptitude tests – you do not need to rehearse and practise in advance, but do remember the following points:

- Listen to any instructions the administrator gives you at the beginning of the session.

- Read any instructions contained in your booklet or on screen.

- Don't waste time reading through the whole booklet and trying to second-guess what the questionnaire is seeking to find out – the test may not be timed, but doing this will not help you or affect your result.

- If the question offers you a 'not sure' or a '?' option, don't resort to this unless you really feel you cannot make a choice.

- Some questionnaires that have a longer rating scale – say 1 to 5, from strongly disagree to strongly agree, or something similar – may advise that you use the extreme ends of the scale only when you feel very strongly. This information will be contained in the written instructions at the beginning of the questionnaire and probably reiterated by the test administrator.

- Do take great care when entering your answers. It sounds obvious, but it is easy to get confused when you are rank ordering from 1 to 5 or ticking a series of either/or options. If you have read several statements that you think are true in your case, it is easy to get into the habit of just ticking the 'true' option.

- Read questions or statements carefully to ensure you understand them.

- Don't spend too long pondering a question and worrying about what to answer – with personality questionnaires it is usually best to go with your first response.

- Answer all the questions – leaving any out will affect your final profile.

- Respond as naturally as you can – don't try to guess which answer you think sounds best.

- Finally, enjoy it – you don't often get a quiet 45 minutes to think about nothing but you!

TEST TROUBLES

Don't be tempted to try to give the answers you think are the good ones. There is no such thing in these personality tests. Besides, a booklet containing anything from 100 to 200 questions will only be looking at four or five traits or 16 to 30 factors, so the same factor or trait is being measured by several different questions, all getting at the same point. It would be impossible as a candidate to unpick all this and there is really no point in trying. Many tests have an impression detector built into their design with questions put there deliberately to measure whether you are trying to convey a certain picture of yourself. Most important of all, you don't know what the 'right' answer is – because there isn't one – so don't waste time trying to guess what it is.

Because you don't pass or fail – or even get a good or a poor score – on a personality questionnaire, giving back meaningful results of personality questionnaires is time consuming and therefore costly. This means at graduate or any other mass job-selection level, candidates are unlikely to be able to get hold of this information. However, if good practice is adhered to, they will be informed of what will happen to their results.

At management development level, it is almost always the case that you will be given your results back with some appropriate and detailed explanation. It may be that what the results reveal indicates a direction in which you could usefully develop within the organization or, conversely, an area where you may require some additional coaching or support.

Examples of the most common types of personality tests

There are many personality assessment tools on the market, but the three listed below are in wide use and also represent some of the different ways in which questions are asked and the range of factors and traits that are measured.

The Myers-Briggs Type Indicator

Based on the work of psychologist Carl Jung, the Myers-Briggs Type Indicator (MBTI) is widely used in occupational and other settings. It is a more popular tool for staff development and training than for selecting new recruits because it offers scope for examining someone's preferred ways of working, rather than offering the kind of assessments provided by some of the trait questionnaires. In this personality assessment you are measured along four independent dimensions:

- **Extroverted or introverted.** Extroverted people have a preference for dealing with the external world – with people, activity and objects. Introverted people are more concerned with the inner world of information and ideas. Extroverts like working with other people and seek variety in their work; introverts like quiet, like to deal with one issue at a time and are happiest working alone.

- **Sensing or intuitive.** Information gathered via the senses is the focus for the sensing person, who also likes to concentrate on the here and now. Those who are intuitive focus on the future, with possibilities and strategies. At work, the sensing person likes to solve practical problems and relies on experience rather than theory to tackle tasks. The intuitive person is far more concerned with the overview and enjoys coming up with new ways of doing things.

- **Thinking or feeling.** Thinking people are logical in the way they consider things and are less interested in social and personal consequences. Feeling people use subjective rather than objective information to reach decisions. Thinking people can be quite critical of others in the work setting and can appear insensitive. Feeling people enjoy working with others, pleasing people and helping others to feel included.

- **Judging or perceiving.** A judging person likes things to be structured and orderly and is very keen on things being properly planned. The perceiving person likes to be spontaneous. The judging person will focus determinedly on a task, sometimes to the exclusion of other things, while the perceiver is capable of being quite flexible. However, the perceiver can be hard to pin down to a particular course of action.

The questionnaire is designed to help people find out how they prefer to look at things and how they prefer to take decisions. The questionnaire comprises just over 80 questions and most of these are the type of question that gives you two options.

Example 5.6

Which of these two statements describes the way you more usually think or feel:

(a) You find it easy to keep a conversation going in almost any situation.

(b) You find it easy to keep a conversation going only with people that you know well.

Example 5.7

Do you usually get on well with people who are either

(a) full of commonsense

or

(b) imaginative.

The questionnaire also contains a section that asks you to choose your preferred word from pairs of words such as 'concrete' or 'abstract', 'hard' or 'soft'.

The results of your questionnaire will be interpreted to produce a profile that places you on each of the four scales (E/I, S/I, T/F and J/P). You will be placed in one of 16 personality types represented by the letter on each scale to which your score is closest.

From reading the brief descriptions of the four scales above, it is easy to see that there is no right or wrong way to be. You can pick out desirable qualities for different work contexts and different working teams for any of the combinations, but you could also come up with some pretty unprepossessing combinations if you tried. The point about the MBTI – and this is true of many other questionnaires – is that they all suggest degrees of behaviour or likely ways of reacting, rather than absolutes.

When used in occupational settings the MBTI indicates people's preferred working styles, but not their only possible working styles. So if you don't like to plan logically but would rather just let things take shape, this does not mean you cannot plan logically, rather that you are less comfortable working in this way. The MBTI is used often in career development counselling at work, or when companies are setting up mentoring and coaching programmes or going through periods of change. The MBTI is also widely applied in fields other than occupational testing – some people who have been through the process are so interested in their profiles that websites have sprung up where you can contact other people with a similar MBTI profile.

The 16-Personality Factor

Versions of the 16-Personality Factor (16PF) questionnaire have been in existence for more than 50 years. It is a very popular personality assessment that is used in selection and development at many different levels.

The 16PF is one of the questionnaires based on trait theories of personality. The standard version consists of nearly 185 questions exploring what sort of person you are. It asks about various subjects, such as your attitudes to other people, what you like doing and how you behave in particular situations. Most of the questions are of the type that give you true/can't say/false answer options.

Example 5.8

I enjoy entertaining people and being the centre of attention.

(a) True   (b) Can't say   (c) False

There are a few questions in the 16PF that look rather more like those you would expect to see in an aptitude test – asking you to pick out relationships between words, find patterns in letters and numbers – but these form only a small section of the test.

The factors that the 16PF measures are:

- warmth
- intelligence
- emotional stability
- dominance
- liveliness
- rule consciousness
- social confidence

- sensitivity
- vigilance
- abstractedness
- privateness
- apprehension
- openness to change
- self reliance
- perfectionism
- tension.

The Occupational Personality Questionnaire

This is another very popular personality tool, especially since it has been designed for use specifically in work settings. It is actually not one questionnaire but a whole group of them and employers can choose the version they think is most appropriate for their situation.

The most popular version of the Occupational Personality Questionnaire (OPQ) has 104 sets of four statements and for each of these you have to state which one is the most like you and which the least. The personality scales on which it assesses candidates are:

persuasive	trusting	democratic
socially confident	achieving	conventional
data rational	independent	forward thinking
adaptable	modest	worrying
rule following	behavioural	affinitive
optimistic	innovative	caring
competitive	relaxed	variety seeking
controlling	emotionally confident	detail conscious
evaluative	decisive	tough minded
conceptual	outspoken	vigorous

The reports produced from scoring on these scales give a detailed profile of the kind of relationships you are likely to have with colleagues, the way you tackle problems, take decisions and plan assignments, how competitive you are – in short, a very detailed profile.

Emotional intelligence

Testing of aptitudes and making assumptions about general intelligence have, and will probably continue to have, their staunch critics. Of course, it is important that an employer knows that any member of staff has the intellectual capabilities for the task in hand, but many employers now think that what is really essential – especially for more key and senior staff – is someone's personal qualities. In 1995 Daniel Goleman, an American psychologist, published his book *Emotional Intelligence*, followed by *Working with Emotional Intelligence* in 1998. His books and ideas found many receptive ears in the worlds of commerce, organizational politics, human resource management and psychology. Business had undergone enormous changes and experienced many new pressures in the two preceding decades and was eager to take a fresh look at what makes people work effectively.

Goleman argues that somewhere between 70 and 80 per cent of success in life, including working life, is attributable to possessing a high EIQ, or emotional intelligence quotient. Emotional intelligence is a combination of being aware of our own feelings and recognizing and understanding the feelings of others. Emotional intelligence enables us to manage and deal with our own emotions and understand how these interact with the emotions of others in our working and other relationships. It also includes the ability to motivate ourselves.

Most emotional intelligence questionnaires measure seven dimensions:

- self awareness – your ability to control and to understand your own feelings;
- resilience – working under pressure and being able to adapt your behaviour to cope with changing demands;

- drive – how much energy and effort you are prepared to put in to achieve your goals;

- sensitivity – being aware of other people's needs and being able to take those needs into account;

- influencing/persuading – how well you are able to get people to agree with your point of view;

- decisiveness – your ability to make unambiguous decisions and not to have to seek too much information to help you take decisions;

- integrity – being able to do what is right and also being able to stick to a course of action once you have embarked upon it.

While all these qualities might be traced back to the 'big five' traits, obtaining a high score on EIQ questionnaires is seen as desirable by many employers – and no doubt many employees who have to work for them, in teams with them, or as their line managers and supervisors. Though less familiar than some personality assessment tools, it seems likely that EIQ measures will continue to grow in popularity with recruiters at every level.

How well do you know yourself?

Whether or not you have completed a personality questionnaire in the past, you will already have an idea of your own personality. On application forms and at interviews – and for every other area of life beyond the world of career planning and job hunting – you will already have a clear idea of what kind of person you are. However, you are rarely asked to think about it in a formal way. Spending a little time considering it won't radically change how you complete a personality questionnaire, but being used to describing yourself may make it feel easier and more comfortable.

Try spending ten minutes writing down a list of as many words as you can that you think describe you. Be honest – don't flatter yourself by putting down words that you would like to apply to you – but don't be too hard on yourself either. Once you have got your list, ask a co-operative friend to write down all the words they think describe you.

Encourage them to be honest (so long as you both feel your relationship is up to it) and then compare the two lists. You are likely to find a fair degree of agreement, but you may make some discoveries if your friend has used words you had never considered might describe you. Sometimes we are good at focusing on one aspect of our personality – perhaps our sociability – because it is openly evident on an everyday basis, but other aspects – like your ability to win an argument without bullying or take a quick decision – may be less visible to you than to others.

You can try this sort of exercise in larger work or peer groups, getting several people to work on one another's lists without seeing what other participants have written. In these instances it is best to insist on a higher number of positive than negative words being included, otherwise the exercise can prove somewhat destructive.

You should to be able to come up with plenty of descriptive words, but here is a short prompt list to get things going:

absent-minded, accommodating, achieving, adventurous, aggressive, agreeable, altruistic, ambitious, amiable, analytical, antagonistic, anxious, argumentative, artistic, assertive, aware, blunt, bold, calm, candid, caring, cautious, changeable, cheerful, competitive, compliant, confident, conforming, conscientious, controlled, controlling, conventional, co-operative, creative, critical, decisive, defensive, democratic, determined, diplomatic, discreet, disorganized, domineering, efficient, emotional, empathic, energetic, enterprising, enthusiastic, experimental, expressive, extroverted, fierce, flexible, forceful, formal, forthright, friendly, gentle, genuine, gregarious, hesitant, hostile, imaginative, impatient, impetuous, impulsive, independent, informal, inhibited, innovative, intolerant, introverted, intuitive, inquisitive, irrational, irresponsible, irritable, jovial, lethargic, logical, loyal, lively, modest, neat, neurotic, obedient, optimistic, organized, outgoing, outspoken, perceptive, perfectionist, persuasive, pessimistic, playful, practical, pragmatic, predictable, private, proactive, quarrelsome, quiet, radical, rash, rational, realistic, reasonable, reflective, relaxed, reliable, reserved, restrained, ruthless, sensible, sensitive, serious, shrewd, shy, stable, steady, stressed, striving, stubborn, submissive, successful, suspicious, temperamental, tenacious, tense, tidy, timid, tolerant, tough, uncompromising, vigilant, vulnerable, warm, willing, yielding, zealous

Even if you don't need this prompt list to help you think about your personality, you might find such a source of words useful in writing or other verbal exercises.

You may also like to have a go at the work-style questionnaire (self-perception inventory) in Part 2 of this book. It is not a personality questionnaire, but it offers some insight into how you are likely to operate in work teams.

As well as personality measures, you may find yourself completing questionnaires about your interests, values, attitudes and work preferences, although sometimes these are not easy to distinguish from personality questionnaires. You are most likely to encounter these as part of a vocational guidance process, but recruiters and selectors may also use them.

Top tips for completing personality questionnaires

- Be careful to follow instructions.

- Be as truthful as you can.

- Work through the questionnaire at a steady pace.

- Don't look for 'right' answers.

- Know yourself well.

6 Selection and development centres

In this chapter:

- Graduate selection centres

- What employers are looking for

- Management development centres

- Applications for managerial jobs

Graduate selection centres and management development centres have been referred to several times in this book so far. But for those who haven't encountered them before, here is an outline of what you might expect.

Graduate selection centres

The selection centre may actually be a physical place, a special company training centre or a hotel with appropriate business facilities. Wherever it takes place, it is an opportunity for employers to put applicants through a range of different selection tests and exercises to gain an overall picture of their suitability for the various positions that are on offer.

Graduate selection centres have become more popular for the same reasons that psychometric tests have gained in popularity – they give some more objective measures of performance than traditional selection procedures and they assess a wider range of attributes in some more 'real work' situations. This is vital in today's world, since graduates are viewed somewhat differently now compared with 15 or 20 years ago. They are expected to display a wider range of life and work skills, to be highly self-motivated and they need to be suitable for fast-tracking.

Attendance at a selection centre may last from one to two days, so it often incorporates an overnight stay and opportunities to socialize and meet members of company staff at mealtimes or during what little free time may be available. While not every selection centre is identical, they are likely to organize a range of the following activities and a typical one will contain all of these exercises.

Interviews

You could face both panel and/or one-to-one interviews. Often the one-to-one interviews are with specialist line managers from the various departments that are recruiting. At the stage where an undergraduate or recent graduate is completing an application form for a company, there are normally openings with different departments – finance, marketing, IT, human resources, product development, etc. Some of these will require specific degree disciplines and particular experience, but many are open to graduates of any subject and applicants may have been asked to rank their preferred choices when they made their applications. Both the interviews and the results of the other tests candidates undergo at the selection centre can determine which of these preferences they are offered.

Aptitude/ability tests

You will be asked to take a range of aptitude tests. Most commonly these will be verbal reasoning, numerical reasoning and diagrammatic reasoning, but – according to specific jobs applied for – others such as perceptual, mechanical and spatial reasoning can also be included.

You will also complete a personality questionnaire, usually one of those based on traits rather than personality type, such as the 16PF or the OPQ mentioned in Chapter 5.

Giving a presentation

You might be asked to give a presentation on a topic that you have been notified of in advance, it might be a topic for which you are given half an hour's notice, or it might be directly linked to another of the exercises you have been asked to do, such as report writing or dealing with an in-tray. Presentations are covered in detail in Chapter 8.

Taking part in a discussion

Once again, this may be linked to other exercises, such as solving a business problem, or role-playing the various members of a committee dealing with an issue or a problem. This is also covered extensively in Chapter 8.

Informal socializing

Many candidates who are asked to attend selection centres find informal socializing one of the most daunting aspects – and this can be just as true for those who would describe themselves as outgoing and confident. Unlike the other selection centre activities, it is unstructured and leaves candidates to make their own decisions about how to behave and react. People get very anxious that specific matters of etiquette are under scrutiny, such as whether you cut your bread roll rather than breaking it, or use a wrong piece of cutlery. It is not really this that is on trial at all – though of course reasonable table manners and courtesy are important. What is being examined is how you cope in situations in which you are meeting a range of new people: whether you are able to make conversation, ask perceptive and penetrating questions, etc. This is because communicating is considered such an important part of so many jobs, although the emphasis placed on your performance in this situation will also vary according to the particular work you want to do.

If you can cast aside your anxieties – definitely without the aid of one too many glasses of the house red – this socializing time can be extremely useful to you. You are meeting potential managers and colleagues and you have a chance to strike up a rapport and create a good impression. This also gives you the opportunity to find out whether you would really like working for this organization. If you find that you feel comfortable with the people you are meeting, you would probably enjoy working alongside them. If you don't find any kindred spirits, maybe this raises doubts for you and helps you to ask some of the questions that matter to you when it comes to your interview sessions. Recent graduate recruits are frequently asked to join in some of these informal sessions and they can tell you more about training, induction and opportunities to move around the company. All this will make you better informed for your interviews and some of the other exercises you will undertake.

What employers are looking for

In the late 1990s the Association of Graduate Recruiters published a report outlining the skills and qualities it felt graduates needed for the twenty-first century. In addition to high levels of verbal, numerical and computer ability, a range of personal qualities was outlined:

- self awareness – able to identify own skills, strengths, values and interests;
- self promotion – able to define and promote own agenda;
- exploring and creating opportunity – able to investigate, identify and seize opportunities;
- action planning – able to organize time efficiently and identify steps needed to achieve a given goal;
- networking – able to develop and maintain networks of contacts that will benefit the organization;
- negotiating – able to reach win–win agreements;
- able to cope with uncertainty – equipped to deal with change in own and organizational situations;
- political awareness – awareness of the internal politics of the com-

pany and the effects external forces have on markets, strategies and developments.

The range of challenges offered at a selection centre has a better chance of assessing potential for some of these qualities than a single interview, however skilled the interview. These qualities are exactly those that a company would expect in its senior staff, so it will try to select for these from the start.

Whether you are attending a selection centre or a management development centre, it is worth reminding yourself of the range of issues that your current or would-be employer is likely to be dealing with and which of these is likely to impinge on your role. This is because the range of tests and exercises you face is likely to be built around such issues. Although even a very intensive two-day test session could not ask you to focus on all of these, employers will be looking for evidence that you have the skills to deal with basic issues, as outlined below.

Dealing with customers

- Dealing with a difficult customer who has no cause for complaint.
- Dealing with a customer who has a valid reason to complain.
- Building relationships with new customers.
- Maintaining good relationships with current customers.

Dealing with staff

- If you are the manager – dealing with a difficult junior colleague.
- Whatever your position – dealing with an awkward colleague who is on the same level as you.
- Coping with a difficult manager – someone whose style does not blend well with your own.
- Working for a manager who does not like to consult.
- Resolving a conflict between two members of staff.

- Resolving a conflict between two departments.
- Disciplining a member of staff.

Counting the cost

- Imposing an unpopular but necessary decision on your staff.
- Working out how to apply cost-cutting measures in your department.
- Working out the balance of cost-cutting measures that will affect several departments.
- Deciding how best to spend allocated funds.
- Putting together a case for receiving additional funds.
- Working out ways to offer good value.

Managing change

- Successfully merging two separate departments into an effective whole.
- Coping if your department is merged with another.
- As a manager – helping your department cope with change.
- Getting your staff to accept an unpopular decision.
- Dealing with an unpredictable situation.

Working in teams

- As a team member – helping your department cope with change.
- Working in a collaborative way with others.
- Developing a good leadership style.
- Getting the best contribution from colleagues.

Motivating and developing staff potential

- Designing and/or implementing a staff appraisal system.
- Looking at your own career development needs and those of others.
- Retaining good members of staff.
- Developing a family-friendly policy.

Good written communication

- Answering a difficult letter.
- Dealing with aggressive e-mails or memos.
- Writing a good, succinct report.
- Turning complex or technical information into something easily understood by a range of colleagues.
- Sifting through a range of information to work out what is really important – seeing the wood for the trees.

Good presentation skills

- Presenting your ideas to a committee or project group.
- Presenting your ideas to customers.
- Successfully chairing a committee or meeting.
- Persuading a person or a group to come around to your point of view.
- Negotiating a successful outcome or deal.

Managing your own work

- Prioritizing your own workload.
- Prioritizing the workload of a team.
- Meeting deadlines.
- Seeing a project through without losing interest.

Management development centres

The essential difference between management development centres and selection centres is that they are not normally used for recruitment. Although the exercises and tests may be used as part of a selection programme, once you move beyond graduate level then organizations are not usually recruiting large numbers of staff at the same time.

Management development centres have been on the increase over the last two decades and look likely to remain a part of the commercial and professional scene for the foreseeable future. During the recessions of the 1980s and 1990s, all types of business had to look at working more efficiently and getting the best value they could from their staff. One way to do this is to look at the ongoing development of staff and see whether they have particular training needs or indeed particular strengths that could be more widely used.

There has also been an increased interest in the personal qualities that go to make up good managers, especially those that can be measured. So there has been a much greater emphasis on a manager's ability to develop team skills and evolve work styles that allow them to be most effective.

Several companies that have carried out surveys asking staff what motivates them to stay and to work hard have found that employees rate good career development and training very highly. Many companies also don't want to lose good staff who might be tempted to work abroad because of better salary or other material benefits. They have found that good, internal career development programmes are a significant factor in staff retention.

These high-level development centres can also enable organizations to work out who is ideal for promotion and to determine to what kind of role they should be assigned. The fact that these programmes are in-house does not mean that they are not competitive. In many instances staff will have to apply to take part in programmes like these and only after successfully completing a detailed written application and interview will they be invited to take part.

So, what might participants in a management development centre expect to encounter? In many ways, the range of activities may be similar to that at a graduate selection centre, but the level will be more sophisticated and more demanding. It will feel very different to a selection centre, because in most instances participants will already have a job and will know many of the other participants. This does not mean that the situation is without potential anxiety and stress. It can sometimes be very difficult to work in circumstances where you are obliged to reveal aspects of your working style and attitudes to colleagues with whom you may feel in competition.

At every level, the development centre is likely to have more sophisticated and more demanding exercises. For example, if you are giving a presentation, it is not likely to be on a topics with titles like 'My Greatest Achievement', but is far more likely to be based on reading complex reports or market information and using this material to put together a good communicative presentation, with many of your working colleagues forming part of the audience.

Personality questionnaires often play a part in development centres and one of the most popular of these is the Myers-Briggs Type Indicator (MBTI), which was covered in more detail in Chapter 5. One of the many good points about development centres is that participants are likely to be given detailed feedback on their performance across the whole range of activities. The feedback can then be incorporated into future career development plans, any apparent training needs can be met and any areas of potential difficulty can be tackled.

Other questionnaires – on management style, level of motivation or work values – may all be incorporated. You will find these questionnaires in Part 2 of this book. These are questionnaires that you can score yourself, so you may find them illuminating.

The 360-degree profile

One tool that is often used, not necessarily in a management development centre but in other career development programmes, is something called a 360-degree profile. This approach can be used in conjunction with various different questionnaires, but its main point is that you are assessed on the same competencies or qualities in four different ways:

- you complete a self-report questionnaire;
- your manager completes a questionnaire;
- members of your team complete a questionnaire;
- a chosen person or group of people, say a particular colleague or chosen colleagues, complete a questionnaire.

In all four cases the questions are the same, to see how close your perception of your work style or the way you relate to others is to the perception of those other groups of people. Questions can be about a range of qualities:

Example 6.1

(a) When a deadline approaches I tend to ...

(b) In a conflict situation I tend to ...

(c) When it comes to listening to other people's ideas I ...

In some versions of this kind of exercise you and the other participants are expected to add your own statements. In others, multiple-choice responses will be offered for all participants to complete.

Example 6.2

When approaching a work deadline I tend to ...

(a) work in the same orderly manner as usual and delegate appropriate tasks to others

(b) become very stressed and irritable with colleagues

(c) enjoy the pressure and keep everybody going

(d) keep myself to myself and get on with it.

Even if your assessors are not using something as sophisticated as the 360-degree profile, peer assessment often forms part of development centres and you may find that colleagues – familiar or unfamiliar – are assessing you on interview performance, how well you give a presentation, what they think of a report you have written and so on. You, of course, will also be joining in assessments yourself and this in itself is a very good teaching exercise.

Taking part in discussions

If you are asked to participate in discussions you are likely to be assigned roles and the subject material is likely to be complex and challenging. You might be divided into two groups, taking the role of representatives from two companies who are discussing a merger. You might be asked to come up with a strategy for implementing a new business plan. You might represent the head of a department and have to work out who should bear the brunt of a reduction in the annual budget and how a 7 per cent saving might be achieved across the board.

In-tray exercises

In-tray exercises are likely to include a great deal of complex data and rely on you having good prioritizing and decision-making skills.

People skills

The greatest focus is likely to be on your 'people' skills. Many people would claim to have good people skills, but what does that mean? It could mean they are:

- good at working in a collaborative way
- good at leading others
- good at motivating others
- good at persuading and negotiating
- good at resolving conflicts
- good at putting others at ease.

You could easily extend this list and these are the kinds of issues that a development centre will look at. The focus may also be on having a really well developed business sense, looking at ways of getting and maintaining competitive advantage and staying ahead in your company's business field.

Sample programme

Outlined below is one typical development centre programme, to give you an idea of what to expect.

Example 6.3

Working in groups of six, you will be given two hours to decide how to spend £1 million for the benefit of the business. Your company has acquired this through selling off one of its chains of Italian-style restaurants and you have to decide which parts of the remaining business could benefit. You have a chain of hotels, a small chain of up-market pubs, a chain of travel agencies and five new leisure complexes. (You would be given data about the performance of each of these groups and you may be allocated a role as representing one of these parts of the business.)

You can appreciate that allocating two hours to this exercise means that you would be expected to go into some detail in working out strategies, advantages, costs, future trends, etc.

Example 6.4

An individual exercise in which you take on the role of a director newly appointed by a market research company. Your task is to interview the head of personnel who has requested a special budget so that she can tackle the problems of low staff morale, high staff turnover and falling productivity rates.

For exercises such as these, an actor will often take the part of an interviewee, so they will have been well briefed about what they should say and also the line they should take, i.e. should they be very determined, aggressive, constructive, pliable, etc. In an exercise like this, it won't necessarily be just your communication skills that are under scrutiny. The business logic that you employ and your attitude to staff training, management of budgets and allocation of new funds, etc. will all be observed and noted.

Example 6.5

A written exercise where you take on the role of a management consultant. A company that runs a small chain of health food stores has called you in to help it develop a business strategy for more effective marketing and hopefully for expansion. It is seeking advice about finance, human resource issues and more effective marketing. You will be given detailed information about the company and allowed an hour and a half to complete this written assignment.

In addition to the above you will have to complete a personality questionnaire and a work-style questionnaire. From these examples you can see that such programmes are very demanding and – as with the graduate selection centres – they offer a range of different exercises designed to reveal your strengths and weaknesses.

Applications for managerial jobs

Selection and development centres are used mainly for graduate jobs and management development programmes but you may also encounter similar tests when you apply for new and more senior jobs as your career progresses. Headhunting agencies, recruitment consultants and individual companies do use tests at these higher levels. They are most likely to use some of the many personality and management style questionnaires available, but they may also use aptitude tests and business analysis/in-tray type exercises.

In these circumstances you should be told in advance what types of test you will be taking and whether you are likely to get results fed back to you. One recruitment consultant who is also an occupational psychologist commented that different companies view psychometric testing of senior managers in very different ways. In some cases, they will set great store by these and even if candidates have done well at interview and have a good track record, if the psychometric tests look at all questionable, they will choose not to employ the individual. Others will pay less regard to the tests if they like the individual and he or she 'feels' right.

You, as an applicant, have no idea about how your prospective employer will react, so all you can do is put as much research and work into preparation as you can. In some cases, if you are applying for this job as a 'one off' and only a small group of candidates is being interviewed at one time, you may be able to obtain more detailed information prior to testing, as well as more detailed feedback.

Top tips for doing well at selection and development centres

- Find out what you can in advance.

- Look upon the activities as an opportunity to learn more about yourself.

- Be prepared for a wide range of different exercises.

- Accept that you are unlikely to perform equally well at everything and play to your strengths.

- For more complex business exercises, prioritizing information is one of the key skills.

- You will have to read, assimilate and act quickly, so if you know this may be a problem, start to practise either in your job or your studies before you are assessed and evaluated.

- Remember, you have already done well to get to this stage, so think positive and be confident.

7 The in-tray, the irate customer and the boss

In this chapter:

- **Real problems need real solutions**

- **Preparing for business exercises**

- **Sample exercises**

Real problems need real solutions

Many selection centres for graduates and development centres for in-company training may ask candidates to solve a range of problems or deal with particular situations that reflect what they are likely to encounter at work. These exercises can form part of any recruitment process, and sometimes just one item or test that is relevant to a particular job may be set for applicants. For example, if someone has applied for a job in customer services they may have to take part in a role-play dealing with a customer on the telephone or in person; or if their job will involve prioritizing large quantities of financial paperwork, they may have to sort through a pile of papers on this subject and decide in what order they would deal with them.

These tests are not psychometric in that they do not measure one candidate against all the others in a quantifiable way, but they are widely used because they provide an insight into how people operate in real work situations. In any case these tests are often set as part of a package that includes aptitude tests.

A true in-tray or in-basket exercise could fill many chapters of one book, since one aim of the exercise is for candidates to sort through a great deal of paper material as quickly as possible, while taking the right decisions and responding to the most important pieces of information. What follows are many of the elements that would make up these exercises, such as dealing with correspondence, writing summaries, organizing information, deciding how to use information, planning workloads and dealing with staffing and customer relations issues.

Preparing for business exercises

- All the psychological and practical preparation outlined in Chapter 3 is relevant again here.

- Think back to work situations where you have had several demands placed on you at the same time and work out where your strategies have been successful and where you would do things differently. Apply this knowledge to your tests.

- Read technical or other complex reports and have a go at summarizing the main points.

- If you don't usually deal with financial reports and budgets, have a look at some of these to become familiar with making quick assessments of financial circumstances.

- Ask colleagues whom you trust to give you candid opinions on how they think you deal with decision making, prioritizing and planning.

- Take a current work or study issue and write a plan of action – even if this is not your usual way of operating.

Sample exercises

The exercises outlined in this chapter are a small sample of the range and type of problems that you may find in business exercises. Topics such as coping with the press, dealing with bad publicity, sorting out disagreements between individuals or departments, designing training programmes, assessing the relative importance of different types of paperwork and looking at financial viability may all feature in the tests you are asked to take. Even if you have not dealt with identical situations at work or in project teams when you were a student, you have probably tackled similar problems at some time in your life, so think back to all the different situations when you have handled problems successfully and use this information to help you.

Tricky complaint letters

Example 7.1

Below is an example of a complaint letter to which you have to formulate a reply.

Dear Sirs

I am writing to complain about my new dishwasher which cost me a lot of money. I was really looking forward to using it and had hoped it would make a big difference.

   I began to feel not very pleased on the day it was delivered. It was not the time of day that I wanted, because I asked if it could be brought early in the morning and the man in the shop said he would do his best, but it might come in the late morning nearer to lunchtime. It arrived at half past two and I had really wanted to go out in the afternoon. I thought that your van would take away my old dishwasher because I cannot get it to the local tip and I was very fed up when your delivery people said they would not take it away. I did not like your delivery people very much as they seemed in a hurry and I wanted them to stay and see that it all worked properly. Now I have had it for three weeks I have found that it does not get things clean when I set it on the economy programme.

> I phoned up and somebody came to look at it, but he said I should have done a wash before he arrived. I think someone did say that on the telephone, but I forgot and anyway if it does not clean things properly it should be up to you to mend it because it is still in the guarantee time. I have been very careful that I put all the right dishwasher stuff in it and I have, so I don't see why it does not work. By the way, the engineer who came to look at it wasn't very smartly dressed and he seemed a bit grumpy.
>
> I hope you can get it sorted out, because I can't tell any of my friends that yours is a good shop to buy their dishwashers.
>
> Yours sincerely
>
> A Paine

You have also been given a copy of a leaflet from your store about the service they provide, so you are able to refer to this before you write your response.

Wonderclean Warehouse – A Promise to Our Customers

If you buy any of our products, we guarantee you satisfaction and an excellent after-sales service. We do our best to deliver the goods at a time that fits in with your busy life; we can give you a date and a promise of morning or afternoon, though it is not possible to be more precise than this. We are sorry, but we are not able to remove old items of equipment for you unless you have arranged a part-exchange purchase. We do guarantee that if you are not completely happy with the product and you let us know about this within 28 days of us delivering and installing it for you, then we shall take the item back and exchange it for you.

The letter from A. Paine arrived at your offices 31 days after the dishwasher had been delivered and installed. Now write a reply to this complaint.

Remember that if you are set a test like this, it is not designed to test your up-to-date knowledge of consumer services law (except in a situation where you have applied for a job as a consumer services officer, or something similar). It is designed to test how you read and consider information, how good you are at using this in your reply and to see whether you are a good communicator, with a good approach to business.

You can either try writing a reply without looking at the following useful hints, or you might like to look at these first to see how they might help you:

- The letter is rambling and not very clear – look for relevant information.

- Separate valid complaints from irrelevant moans.

- Decide whether there are any issues which you, as a company, have to address.

- Think about making your language clear and understandable to your recipient.

- Ensure that you are not admitting responsibility for things for which you are not responsible.

Learning to be brief

Example 7.2

You work for a hotel that is about to launch its new conference facilities, and you have to provide some general information for a press release. You can't crib from a brochure, because it has not been printed yet, so all you have are various pieces of information to bring together into a 150-word piece:

- The hotel is based around an eighteenth-century manor house, but the conference suite is a new development.

- The new facility offers a 100-place lecture theatre and four meeting rooms, which can each hold up to 15 people.

- Latest audio-visual aids are available.
- Facilities can be booked on a daily basis.
- Exhibition space is available.
- Overnight accommodation is available.
- A full range of catering services is available, including special diets, business breakfast and banquet menus.
- There are pleasant and spacious grounds in the heart of the English country-side – ideal for relaxation and enjoyment.
- A full range of leisure facilities is available.
- Early booking is advised.
- Prices are competitive.

As you work on combining all these facts into a readable and informative press release:

- Work out what information is most important.
- What makes it sound interesting?
- Are there any unique selling points?
- Make it easy to read.

Responding to complex information

Here is an exercise where several documents are presented to you and you have to respond accordingly. This exercise does not rely on your knowledge of the planning procedure or environmental law, central or local government policy – you are not being tested on these. Instead, you are being tested on your ability to assimilate information and viewpoints from different sources and then to come up with a good, clear response.

Example 7.3

You work in the public relations department of a property development company, which has recently applied to build 50 new homes on the edge of a village with a current population of around two thousand people. You have been asked to provide a written report for a local council meeting and you have been given a range of documents to consider before putting together your response.

Managers' brief

Your brief from your own managers is that they are committed to the development going ahead, they are optimistic about it getting planning agreement, but they do not want to become too unpopular with the local community or complicate the debate for any longer than necessary. They want you to represent them as responsible and sympathetic, but determined to get this project off the ground.

2 A letter, accompanied by a petition signed by 600 people

Dear Sirs

It is with great concern that we have learned of your plans to build 50 new homes on the edge of this village. While we fully accept that there is a need for new housing and we understand that every area must take a share in this, we have doubts as to the merit of this particular development.

So far, we have been unable to obtain information as to what percentage of this housing will be low cost and therefore affordable to members of our own community. We understand that many of the properties will be three and four-bedroom luxury accommodation, which is not the kind of property that we need in this area.

We are approaching the local council to enquire what additional health and education facilities may be developed here, since the local school is already full to capacity and there is also limited local transport available.

We would appreciate it if you would reconsider your plans and would also welcome the opportunity to discuss either a reduction in the proposed number of properties and/or some clearer information outlining the exact proposals on low-cost housing.

Yours faithfully

3 A letter from a group of small businesses

Dear Sirs

We understand that you are planning to build 50 new homes adjacent to the village of Wildbury West and would like to state our general support for this development, which we hope will bring additional work and finance into the area. We represent a group of small businesses in the area – in fact 92 per cent of businesses in the village and surrounding countryside belong to our association. We represent a range of businesses – shops, caterers, all the building trades, landscape architects, horticulture and a little light industry – and we welcome the possibility of more customers and a potential increased volume of business being brought into the area.

We are, however, concerned that such developments as the one you propose, which bring in those who don't have a sense of identity with the area, may simply encourage new residents to travel to larger towns to shop or to seek other services that could be provided locally.

We wondered whether you have considered any initiatives – such as using local skills and local labour – in your development, and whether you have any other ideas for initiatives that will help the area to thrive and maintain quality of life for the new residents in your homes, as well as the current local community.

Yours faithfully

4 An article from a local newspaper

New homes or no homes, that is the question.

Once again a property developer threatens to build another blot on our fast disappearing local landscape. The *Wildbury Gazette* has exclusive information that the new housing development will take little account of the needs of our young people waiting to settle down and raise a family in our own locality, and still less account of older people who would like to buy a comfortable little house or bungalow and remain living close to their families.

We can expect our roads to become death traps, with fast expensive cars whizzing through the village, taking no account of children or walkers or cyclists. Many of the houses will probably be empty all day or even all week, until their owners deign to return on a Friday evening. Then they will spend the weekend complaining that they have been woken by cockerels or that their dinner parties have been ruined by farmland smells.

When is our council going to take a stand, and when, Mr Fat-Cat Developer, are you going to have the courage to come and talk face to face with the community that you are so happy to ignore?

The *Wildbury Gazette* would welcome some comments from the company, but no one has wanted to talk to us so far.

5 A report on the suitability of the land for development

A short report from land surveyors, which suggests that there are no serious problems in building on this land – it is not in an area prone to flooding and there are no potential problems with the type of buildings or the construction methods proposed.

6 A memo from your director

Please find copies of the enclosed papers concerning the Wildbury West Development. I would like you to prepare a short written report that can be presented at the next meeting of the local council and which makes the point that subject to full planning approval the development will go ahead. You may wish to know that eight of the proposed homes will be in the low-cost starter-home bracket.

Give yourself 45 minutes to write a short report that you would like to be presented at the meeting.

■ Have a quick, initial glance through each item so that you quickly gain an overall picture.

■ Decide whether there is anything you can afford to ignore.

■ Work out what points you need to get across.

■ Organize the material to work out who is for and who against the development, so that you know exactly whom you are addressing.

■ Decide whose concerns you should address.

■ Look for common concerns or statements of support in the different items.

■ If there are areas of difficulty, decide when and how to tackle these.

■ Work out an introduction and a conclusion.

■ Keep an eye on the time.

■ Ask yourself whether you could answer questions on what you have written and maintain the line you have developed.

Resolving a staff conflict situation

Example 7.4

You are the manager of a team of staff in your company's systems support department. You have two reception staff who deal with all initial personal and telephone enquiries. Mark has worked in the department for some time: he is a popular member of the team and gets on well with people, but he has a rather disorganized way of working, so that if anyone else takes over at his work station, they find an odd mix of notes and messages on screen. However, he knows what he is doing, although if he is on holiday or unwell life can be chaotic and things do sometimes get forgotten. Theresa is new to the department and has excellent organizational and administrative skills, although she is not especially liked by colleagues. She gets the job done well and is polite and very efficient when dealing with enquiries. Sometimes she is a little sharp with people if they are not very clear at explaining the difficulty they are having.

One morning, when everything appears to be running smoothly, you suddenly become aware that Mark and Theresa are having a blazing row in the middle of the office. What steps do you take to resolve the situation?

Spend 15 minutes writing a brief outline of the steps you would take to deal with the immediate crisis and what measures you would adopt to ensure the problems did not happen again.

You may like to do this exercise without reading on, or you may prefer to look at the hints about what you need to consider.

- Should you stop the immediate situation – removing the arguing staff from customers, from colleagues and from one another?
- Should you give them both some time to calm down before you deal with the situation?
- Is it appropriate to refer to the company's disciplinary procedures?
- How quickly would you arrange separate meetings with each of them?
- Would you discuss the issue with other staff in the department who witnessed the start of the quarrel?
- Would you arrange a meeting for the two of them to talk things through together?

- Would you choose to be at that meeting?
- What do you consider are Mark's main working strengths?
- What are Mark's weak points and what would you suggest he does to improve these?
- What are Theresa's working strengths, and how would you capitalize on these?
- What are Theresa's weaknesses and what would you suggest she does to improve them?
- What measurable outcomes would you set to ensure that improvements take place?
- What time frame would you set to review the situation?

TEST TROUBLES

For some exercises involving conflicts or a difficult customer, you will be asked to role play, rather than complete a written exercise. On some occasions it may be other candidates or participants who take on the role of frustrated customer or irate manager, but on other occasions actors will be employed, so that the line they take can be very clearly dictated to provide a more controlled measure of how you react.

This is very different to working out a problem on paper, but familiarizing yourself with strategies to deal with difficult situations will help you to give a better impression in a role play. In these situations always:

- listen to what the other person is saying;
- don't rush in with your replies or comments – take a few moments to consider;
- never lose your cool – the exercise is probably designed to see how you cope under stress and provocation.

One of those days

This is an exercise that asks you to look at someone's work situation and identify ways in which they might operate differently and more effectively.

Example 7.5

Read through the situation below and identify what you think would be better responses for Jim to make to show he is in control and is managing himself well.

It is 1.30 pm and Jim is due to attend a project review meeting in half an hour. The previous meeting was held two weeks ago and Jim had agreed that he would follow up a number of small items for the group. Jim reaches for his file and starts going through his papers. As he reads, his mind starts to race as he sees the items in the minutes that he said he would follow up.

He hastily turns to his PC and starts to compose e-mails that will get some of the jobs started. He manages to get three out of four done and then looks at his watch. It is 2 o'clock. Jim turns away from his unfinished e-mails and rushes off to the meeting.

The group works through the items agreed last time. Jim explains that he has not quite finished the ones he undertook because the finance manager asked for some figures to be produced in a hurry and his secretary had been tied up with that job, so Jim's work for the project group had taken second place – it would definitely be done today or tomorrow.

The group moves on to discuss the part of the project for which Jim is responsible. This involves organizing internal staff training on using a new system. Tim, a colleague of Jim's, expresses some concerns about the staff attitude towards training. Jim quickly steps in as he feels Tim's comments are unfair. He points out the lengths he has gone to to make sure that staff understand the background to the project and he says he believes all is going well on the training front. He adds that if Tim does not agree, perhaps he would like to try taking over the training. After Jim has finished speaking there is a silence in the group. Jim feels slightly awkward, but thinks that Tim should not have criticized him in front of the group. There will always be some staff who have a negative attitude to training – and in any case, what was the evidence on which Tim was basing his comments?

The meeting moves on to other topics on the agenda and Jim does not take much interest. He is still irritated by what Tim said and their conversation is running through his head, blocking out the discussions of the group.

At the end of the meeting Jim returns to his office and thinks, 'Thank goodness that's over – now what was I doing?'.

Before looking at the following comments, try writing down a few short paragraphs about how Jim might work more effectively.

Jim appears to have several problems:

- He is feeling stressed by different work demands and not coping well.

- His time management is poor – he has not looked at the file until half an hour before his meeting and this does not give him enough time to do anything properly.

- He has several communication problems in the meeting – he makes excuses for why he has not followed up his tasks.

- He gets very defensive about staff training.

- He is hostile to Tim and his attitude makes the whole group feel uncomfortable.

- He misses opportunities to contribute to parts of the discussion where he is not under pressure, because he is still wound up about his discussion with Tim.

- His concentration is poor because of all the factors above, so he does not have a clear plan of action when he returns to his office.

Jim could take several steps to work more effectively:

- He could have set aside specific time after the first meeting to follow up the items to which he had agreed. Notice there was no mention of Jim possessing a diary.

- He would then have been able to decide which of his four e-mails was the most important – then even if time had not allowed him to complete all of them, he would probably have had at least one or two responses by now.

- He could have apologized more directly to the rest of the group, rather than half blaming his secretary.

- He could have responded far less defensively to Tim, for instance simply asking him calmly what evidence or examples he had of the negative attitudes to training.

- Even if he felt uncomfortable about what he had not done, he could have joined in the other discussions in the meeting and made useful contributions, rather than switching off because of his own irritation.

- When he returned to his office he should have made an immediate plan for how to progress matters before the next meeting.

- He could have gone and had a private word with Tim to forge a better working relationship, rather than allowing the hostility to fester.

These are the sorts of answers you would be expected to come up with.

What shall I do first?

Example 7.6

You left work on Friday night and started a course at a nearby hotel on Monday morning. The course lasts for one week. At 12.30 pm on Wednesday, the tutor passes you a message asking you to return to your department as soon as possible. From what you can make out, the message is from a colleague who you try to phone, but you keep getting her voicemail. Before you left on Friday, you handed everything over to Pat, but from the message you understand that she has gone home feeling unwell.

You decide to excuse yourself for an hour since the group is about to break for lunch. You return to the office and are faced with eight situations. Prioritize these in the order you would be likely to deal with them.

1 There is a note on your desk saying that Lisa has been offered a job with another company. She wants to talk to you as soon as you return and you calculate that this discussion will only take about 15 minutes. Lisa is one of the most valuable members of your team.

2 Your telephone is indicating that there are messages on your voicemail.

3 You just know that when you switch on the computer there will be about 50 e-mail messages waiting for you. The irritating thing is that about half of them will be bulletins that are not relevant to you. Experience has shown that it will only take about five minutes to delete these and you might stumble across some really urgent e-mails in the process.

4 A note is stuck to your screen. It is from your manager asking to see you as soon as you return. It is not dated. Your meetings with your manager are usually 30 minutes minimum.

5 A member of your team has seen you coming into the building and is sitting at your desk. As you approach, they ask if you have got 10 minutes.

6 One of the company directors has left a message with Pat saying that he would like to see you and could you telephone his secretary to make an appointment as soon as you return. Pat has left this message on your desk.

7 Pat's telephone is ringing on a neighbouring desk; she has clearly forgotten to switch the voicemail on.

8 Because you rushed away from the training course just before lunch, you have not eaten. You are really hungry, but realize that it will take about 15 minutes

to go up to the dining room and eat a decent meal. There are no other facilities available.

Write down the order in which you would do these things, being sure to include all eight items.

For this exercise, just as for many others that you will meet during the selection process, there are no necessarily 'right' answers. However, there are certain things you should consider:

- the time allocation for the different situations;
- any prior knowledge you have about these situations;
- which items might unsettle you if you don't deal with them;
- what the expectations of the other people involved might be;
- which situations might lead to further complications that have the potential to tie you up for even longer.

There is no perfect response, but some of the following points are worth bearing in mind:

1 **The situation with Lisa.** Lisa is a valued member of the team and you only know that she has been offered a new job, not that she has accepted it. The time you are prepared to spend discussing this with her may have some influence on the decision she makes, as might your attitude to being able to give her time at the moment. On the other hand, she might be planning to take the new job whatever and only wants to discuss it with you out of courtesy, so why make this a priority?

2 **Voicemail messages.** Presumably you set your voicemail to let people know you would be out all week, so if they wanted to contact you urgently, they should have found another means of getting through to you. Some voicemail messages can take a long time to deal with, especially if you have to write down details and contact numbers.

3 **E-mail messages.** E-mails have the advantage over telephone calls that you don't have to engage with them if you don't want to – you

can delete irrelevant ones and there is no need to copy down any information. There is always the chance that one of the e-mails will give you some clues about the other situations you are tackling.

4 **Your manager.** It is a good work practice and a natural instinct to know what your manager wants. However, in this situation, the manager probably knows you are away for the week and is not anticipating meeting with you until your return. The fact that the note is undated tends to suggest this, although it does not offer certainty.

5 **Your team member.** It is difficult to turn away someone who is sitting by your desk, but on the other hand he is being a bit of an opportunist, who just happened to see you enter the building. Perhaps you could combine having lunch with a meeting with this team member, thus dealing with two items on the list at the same time and again creating a possible opportunity to pick up other information.

6 **The director.** The information you have been given tells you nothing about the size of the company – in a large company it is unlikely that the company director will be aware of your comings and goings. A quick telephone call to his PA will enable you to set a meeting at the time that suits you.

7 **Pat's ringing telephone.** There is no reason why you should answer the telephone, but is it going to interrupt your other important work? Can you answer it and be brief with the caller and at least set the voicemail so that the rest of your hour is spent in peace?

8 **Lunch.** Lunch may seem a luxury amidst the rush, but will you be able to concentrate on your course or any other tasks in hand if you are distracted by hunger? Could you combine it with a meeting with your team member or a meeting with Lisa?

It is still up to you to choose the rank order. When groups of people do this exercise, invariably different rank orderings emerge. If the paper exercise is combined with a discussion, more than one working order can be logically explained and justified.

Why is everybody leaving?

This is a problem-solving exercise where it is your job to improve the situation.

Example 7.7

You have just been appointed as manager of a customer services department for a financial organization. Customers can call by telephone or come in person and the department is always very busy. When you take over, you are managing a staff of 22; you have two assistant managers and everyone else is on the same level, though some are more experienced than others.

You have been told by the three senior staff who appointed you that one of your tasks is to bring down both staff sickness and staff turnover – both of these are running at 25 per cent higher than in any other part of the company. You are not given a specific time limit in which to achieve these goals, but you get the feeling you are supposed to have an impact quickly.

You look at the structure of the department: yourself, two deputy managers and 19 customer services staff. You look at the working hours and see that everybody works from 9.00 am to 5.00 pm with customer contact hours being 9.15 am to 5.00 pm. The atmosphere in the department seems pleasant – although people are clearly very busy, they all seem to get on fairly well and any personality clashes appear to be very minor.

Both your deputy managers have been in post less than a year and seem to be becoming a little despondent. You conduct brief interviews with all the staff and they all complain about pay. While it may be human nature to want more money, this does seem to be a very strong feeling. You are not going to make yourself popular by suggesting to your new managers that they substantially increase their salary bill, so what other steps might you take to motivate your staff?

Before looking ahead, make a note of some of your own suggestions. Then see whether there is any similarity between your suggestions and the list below:

- Introduce a flexitime system – this would benefit customers and also give staff some options and choices about different ways of working.

- Examine the induction programme that staff are given and see whether it prepares them well enough for the work ahead.

- Look at ways of altering people's workload so that they have more breaks from customer contact while providing back-up administrative support for colleagues.

- Create some team leader posts for staff to lead teams of four or five, so that there is a further level for career development and a chance for more staff to develop some new supervisory skills.

- Introduce more staff training and development for the department.

- Introduce a staff appraisal system.

- Begin a systematic series of exit interviews when staff do leave, so that you can collect data.

- Review the staff sickness monitoring procedure in the department.

- Have meetings with the staff groups or teams to get feedback from them on where problems are arising.

An exercise like this could be set as a pencil and paper exercise, but it could also be done in a way that asks you to discuss it with other participants afterwards, or you may be interviewed and asked to justify your responses.

Effective marketing

Example 7.8

You work for the marketing department of a chain of hotels, which has just decided to market some new and different types of weekend break. The company produces more than one brochure and your task is to allocate the weekend breaks to the brochures you feel they fit most appropriately.

The breaks on offer are:

1 **Wild West.** Two-day introductory courses in Western style horse riding, with an evening barn dance and barbecue. Courses are suitable for horse riders of any standard, from novice to advanced. Price band 4.

2 **Green and Pleasant Land.** Two or three-day breaks for everyone. Based in hotels in the heart of the countryside, with opportunities to follow nature trails, go on guided rambles and attend lectures on local wildlife. Optional visits to local places of historic interest. Special children's events included. Suitable for children aged seven and upwards. Price band 3.

3 **Let Your Hair Down.** Based at hotels in the centres of some of the liveliest cities in the country. Within walking distance of all the shops and the vibrant nightlife of restaurants, clubs, cinemas and casinos. Price band 2.

4 **Stress Breaker.** At hotels that offer extensive leisure facilities, including swimming pools, saunas, spa pools and health clubs. Activities on offer include yoga, aromatherapy, massage and exercise programmes. Price band 5.

5 **Meet New People.** Special weekends for those who enjoy the luxury of eating fine food in pleasant surroundings, attending the theatre, visiting places of interest, or simply good conversation. Designed for people who want to enjoy all this, but feel a bit reticent about being on their own. Price band 2.

6 **Golden Age.** Offered at several hotels, these breaks include evening cabaret entertainment and excellent full-board menus. Optional events include bridge, ballroom dancing and visits to local places of interest. Hotels offering these breaks are within easy access of the centre of town, but not right in the heart of the city. Price band 4.

7 **Utter Luxury.** Offered at the most exclusive hotels, all of which have excellent restaurants, extensive wine lists and superb leisure facilities. A range of additional sports and leisure activities can be organized, including gliding lessons, horse riding, water skiing, golf and much, much more. Price band 5.

8 **Nice and Easy.** Economy breaks for all the family at a wide range of hotels in city and country locations. All hotels have swimming pools and some have special children's play areas. Babysitting available and lots of information on things to do and places to go. Price band 1.

The different brochures are:

1 **Family Breaks** – showing the full range of breaks suitable for all the family.
2 **Relax and Enjoy** – contains a range of the more expensive breaks on offer and is aimed at the 25–50-year-old market.
3 **Wild Times** – outlines the breaks that are aimed at the 18–35-year-old consumer.
4 **Time's Pleasures** – aimed at the 50-years-plus consumer.

It is quite possible to allocate a holiday to more than one brochure, but you should ensure that you have allocated them all to at least one brochure.

The key to solving problems like this is that the information you are given is normally full of clues – price bands, references to children, description of location, etc. – so it is not too difficult to work out what should go where. However, you will be working against the clock and for a comparatively simple exercise like this you would be allocated only ten minutes at most, possibly less.

Comparing options

You may be asked to consider different proposals and decide which is the best option. You must do this by providing a written report.

Example 7.9

Two million pounds of funding has been allocated as a contribution towards a tourist development that is to be based around a new science theme park, with exhibitions, activities and interactive displays about science and the natural world.

Businesses are expected to come up with the major part of the cost and there are three proposals on the table for you to consider.

Option 1 Company 1

Company 1 has allocated £20k for the project and it would like to build the complex in an area of the country that has no other major tourist attractions of this kind.

Plus points:

■ Land is relatively cheap in this area.

■ There is fairly high unemployment in the area and this development will create employment.

■ There is some very enthusiastic local support, mainly because of the employment issue.

■ The company has a good track record on completing projects on time, though it has not always managed to remain within budget.

Minus points:

■ The area is relatively remote so there may not be the appropriate infrastructure of road and rail networks to bring people to the area – and these are extra costs not covered in the company's plan.

■ There is some environmental opposition because the proposed site is close to a site that is an important nature reserve and there is concern that wildlife will be disrupted.

■ There is some worry about how extra funds will be raised if the company does not remain within budget.

■ Traffic congestion could be a concern on minor roads.

Option 2 Company 2

This company proposes to develop the facility on the edge of a city. It has £30k to invest in the project.

Plus points:

- There are very good links for rail and particularly for road because the site is very close to a major motorway.
- The company is willing to put up £30k, which is a larger contribution than Company 1.
- There is local support for the project from the business community.
- Company 2 is a very reliable company with a good record on keeping to cost and meeting completion targets.
- The potential labour force will be easy to find, from management through to specialist and casual workers.

Minus points:

- Land prices are relatively expensive here.
- Although close to the city, it is a green field site.
- There is already a major sports complex nearby, so perhaps the development would bring too much traffic into the area.
- Residents who live closest to the site are concerned about the size of the development and the amount of car parking that will be needed.

Option 3 Company 3

This is a new company, which plans to invest £18k on the development, close to a medium sized town.

Plus points:

- The company will build on the site of a group of old warehouses and so improve a very dilapidated area.
- The site is close to a major road network and railway station, although not that close to a motorway.
- There is warm local response for the development, including approval from the environmental lobby and community groups, which would like to see the area improve.

■ One or two other major attractions are available within a 50-mile radius, so the development may be effective in bringing more tourists into the whole area.

Minus points:

■ Land is relatively expensive here, although not as expensive as the city site, and the company's smaller investment would only allow for a more modest development.

■ There is no motorway link, so traffic congestion could be a problem.

■ This is a new company, so there is no proven track record to take into account.

Spend 30 minutes writing your own proposal. Set out your arguments for whichever option you choose and also show which would be your second and your third choices.

When writing reports like this:

■ Take all the factors into account.

■ Follow your arguments through logically and deal with anticipated counter arguments, even though this is a paper rather than a discussion exercise.

■ Ensure that your writing is clear and concise – stick to short sentences and short statements.

■ Try to deal with one major point per paragraph.

■ Write a definite conclusion.

Top tips for dealing with business exercises

■ Listen to any instructions you are given at the beginning of the session.

■ Read any written instructions carefully.

■ In contrast to the advice for many aptitude tests, here it is good to look at every piece of information provided, so long as you don't get caught up in reading anything lengthy.

- Check quickly for summaries of information, financial details, ideas on who else you might delegate something to, etc.

- Note any key points as you go along, so that you don't have to waste time reading things a second time.

- Look for hints contained in the information.

- Keep a very strict eye on the clock. Some exercises with a lot of paperwork may allocate you an hour or longer, but you should still use your time carefully.

- Keep calm and confident – your behaviour as well as your answers may also be assessed.

8 Talk your way to success

In this chapter:

■ Communication skills tests

■ Presentations

■ Presentation fundamentals

■ Topics for presentations

■ Discussions

■ Effective participation

Communication skills tests

Taking a test does not only mean sitting down in an examination-type situation and going through a question paper. Employers of all kinds and at many levels state that one of the skills they most desire in their employees is the ability to communicate effectively. Many of us say on our CVs 'I am a good communicator', but being a successful communicator actually covers a range of communicating skills. Good communication includes:

■ being able to express yourself clearly and succinctly on paper;

■ translating complex legal or technical information into everyday language;

- presenting an idea to a group of people;
- persuading a person or a group to buy something, do something or come around to your point of view;
- listening carefully to what is being said by others;
- encouraging other people to make a contribution to discussions.

These skills will all draw on good verbal reasoning ability, which may be measured by aptitude tests, and a range of personal qualities, which may be measured either by personality questionnaires or by special exercises designed to see how candidates perform in 'real' situations.

This chapter examines some of the exercises that test communication skills. Report writing skills and some of the techniques for testing good one-to-one communication were covered in Chapter 7.

Presentations

A presentation might be required of graduate applicants seeking entry to a wide range of professions. It will also often form part of the programme of tests that middle and senior staff are put through at development centres. The topic and the depth you will be expected to go into will inevitably be less at graduate level than for senior managers.

Consider how many real work situations require this skill and you can see why it is a much used test. Teaching a class of students, presenting a new product or service idea to a sales team, running a staff training session for new recruits, presenting annual turnover figures to a board of directors, giving evidence to a parliamentary committee, prosecuting or defending a case in court, giving information to a group of holiday makers about their resort and the facilities on offer – the list is endless.

Many readers will be quite familiar with either giving presentations themselves or sitting through those given by others, and will therefore have clear perceptions of what works and what doesn't. You know what keeps your attention and what causes surreptitious glances at your watch, or what inspires you and what leaves you thinking about the pile of work in your in-tray that you had to abandon to attend this event. However, you should still prepare carefully before any and every presentation.

Recruiters will take different approaches to asking you to give a presentation. They will almost always give you a warning that you will have to do this, but the topic upon which you present may be either chosen by you or it may be something selected for candidates by employers. If the topic is notified in advance, this advance may be as far ahead as being part of your letter of invitation, or it may be just 20–30 minutes beforehand, as a further test of your ability to organize information. At senior management level, it is likely that a topic will be chosen for you and that you will be given a more complex range of information to work on.

Remember that this exercise is not designed to humiliate you and make you jump through unnecessary hoops. It is designed to test a skill that will be needed for the position to which you are applying and to provide some measure of how you are likely to cope in a potentially stressful situation. If you have to choose a topic, you have the freedom to choose a subject that you will enjoy speaking about. On the other hand, if you are allocated a topic then you don't face the agonizing decision of whether you have selected something appropriate – and you know that other candidates have been allocated the same subject.

Whatever the subject you are talking on, the length of time you have been allocated to speak, the time you have been given to prepare, or the level of career entry or career development at which you are participating, there are some fundamental guidelines that will always apply.

Presentation fundamentals
Structure your information

If you are still in education, or have recently left college, school or university, you will be well aware that any essay, project or other assignment has to have a structure. Any project needs an opening that sets the scene, some interesting content that follows a logical pathway, and a conclusion that is related to what has gone before. The same applies to any presentation. Whether your presentation lasts for 5 minutes or 30 minutes, it must follow a structure.

Organize your material

Organize yourself by working out the main points that you want to get across. Don't go for too many of these – between three and six is probably enough. Don't be like one much quoted Oxford don who was overheard turning to a somewhat weary looking colleague and saying 'and eleventh'. Our capacity to retain too much new information is limited, even though it varies from one individual to another.

Control your voice

The importance of good control of your breathing was mentioned in Chapter 3, on preparing to take tests. In the public arena, when you are speaking to a group, mastering your breathing is essential – not just for the preparation, but for the delivery too.

Actors, singers and those who play wind instruments learn a great deal about how to use their breathing both to improve the quality of their voices (or sound of their instruments) and to control nerves and anxiety. Many businesses that offer their staff presenting skills training will include a mini version of such breath training as part of that course.

However, you can practise much of it without ever attending a course.

Lie down on the floor in some private place. Begin breathing deeply and place one hand on your lower abdomen. You should be able to feel your abdomen pushing against your hand as you breathe in and then sinking as you breathe out. The point of this exercise is that most of us don't use the total capacity of our lungs. On average we use only about a third of our lung capacity and this tends to be the top third, which inevitably makes our voices sound more nasal and less resonant. As a bonus, this kind of deep abdominal breathing really does help you to feel in control.

Think also about making your voice sound interesting. Modulate it rather than speaking in a monotone – put some feeling into what you are saying. There is a very good exercise to help develop this, which you can do with a friend. Ask them to sit down with their back to you, so that they cannot see your facial expressions. Pick a list of neutral words, perhaps the numbers one to ten, or nothing that is likely to provoke humour. Say those neutral words in a very soft voice, no more than a whisper, but try to put some feeling like enthusiasm, concern or delight into those words. Note beforehand which words you are going to use to convey which emotions and then get your partner to write down their responses and see how well they coincide with yours.

Speak at a good strong volume

Correct breathing will also help you to speak more loudly without shouting. It is very easy – especially when you are nervous – to speak softly, but if your audience can't hear what you are saying you have immediately lost them. Always check that everybody can hear you – ask them once you have given some very brief introduction such as 'Good morning, today I am going to talk about our latest product launch …'. Checking that your audience can hear you not only serves a practical purpose but immediately lets them know this is a two-way event – you are interested in their experience, as well as wanting to put across your own points.

One actor who runs training courses says that if you think of the volume of your voice as being on a scale of 1 to 6, when you are speaking to a group you should always aim to have the volume dial at 4. You may often feel that this is too loud – if you are the speaker – but for your audience this makes things easy for them to hear. It also conveys the notion that you are confident about what you are saying – and that you feel it is worth hearing.

Use prompt notes

Don't read from a script – it sounds boring, it stops you making eye contact with your audience, and in fact it really stops you engaging with them at all. However, it's fine, indeed wise, to have prompt notes. These are most easily handled if they are a written on small cards –

index cards or blank postcards are ideal. You should number these, so that in the unlikely event of you dropping them all, you can easily put them back in order without your presentation falling apart.

TEST TROUBLES

There is a tendency to speak far too quickly when you are giving a presentation, often because you are anxious or feel that you must cover everything. Make a conscious effort to slow down – your audience will find it easier to absorb what you are saying, easier to ask questions (if you have invited them to) and you will appear much more confident.

Use visual aids

Your options to use visual aids will vary, but in many situations, especially at management development level, you may have a full range of equipment available to you, including PowerPoint, OHP, flip charts and white boards. There is no rule that says that because everything is available you have to use it all. It is, however, reasonable to assume that if visual aids equipment has been made available to you then you should use some of it. Bear in mind that different members of an audience respond differently – some people really like visual information, others concentrate more on what you are saying. By offering both words and visual aids you have the chance of winning the attention of most of your audience.

Watch the time

Keep an eye on the time. When you are planning your presentation you should make sure that you deliver it at a moderate pace in the time allowed, with a few minutes to spare, so that if there are any questions or interruptions you can take this in your stride without having to miss out sections of what you planned to say. It is not a bad idea to have one optional section in your presentation, which you can either miss out or include, according to how time is going. Remember that where presentations are being given as part of a selection process the time-keeping tends to be very strict – you may even be cut off in mid-sentence.

Top tips for giving a good presentation

- Think about your audience first.

- Use whatever planning time you have as effectively as you can.

- Use appropriate visual aids.

- Make sure your presentation has a clear starting point and summary, as well as worthwhile contents in between.

- If you have the opportunity, do a test run to check that you can keep to a time limit.

- If you are able to prepare your presentations well in advance, do this test run with an audience, friends, colleagues – or even your cat.

- Prepare a set of cue cards – leave the copious notes behind.

- Enjoy what you are talking about.

- Try not to get flustered if things go wrong – coping in adverse circumstances can gain you marks. Losing your thread or dropping your prompt cards doesn't mean you have failed – bursting into tears or running out of the room probably does.

- Thank people for listening.

Topics for presentations

Here are some examples of topics that have been set as subjects for presentations at graduate selection level:

- The achievement of which I am most proud.

- How I set about planning an assignment.

- This interests me – I hope it interests you too.

- Getting people to work well together.
- The customer is always right.
- Good reasons to become a … [whatever the position applied for].
- Business studies [or any other subject that you have been studying] is a really useful subject.
- Staying one step ahead of your competitors.
- Taking a year off to travel puts you behind on the career ladder.
- How university education should be funded.
- How I would solve London's transport problems.
- The impact of e-mail on business communications.

Unless you are specifically asked to speak about your course, it is a good idea to think of something different – think about talking about a decision, an achievement or an interest. The chances are that other candidates will also be tempted to resort to talking about their studies as a good, safe option, so even though you may present it incredibly well, if yours is the twelfth talk on the same subject even the most fair-minded and scrupulous assessor may be affected by the boredom factor.

Employers will not ask you to speak on overtly political topics, but they may ask you to speak about things that do not necessitate you revealing your party politics – how you see Britain's role in Europe, factors to consider in a good environmental policy, the impact of global markets on a particular sphere of employment, etc.

As well as the general topics listed above, you may be asked to give a presentation that relates directly to your presentation. For example, someone applying for a job as a trainee teacher might be asked to talk about planning an interesting lesson, a trainee lawyer might be asked to talk about the extensive use of the Human Rights Act, or a would-be project manager about how they would manage a particular project.

When someone is asked to give a presentation at middle and senior management level, whether as part of an application procedure or as part of a management development programme, the topics are far more likely to relate directly to the business concerned. They are also more likely to be based on reading material beforehand and presenting a report on what you have read. (Chapter 6 gives more information on development centres.)

Discussions

Being asked to participate in a discussion of some kind is a very common activity during selection and development centres. For many professions, working well with groups of people is important – for example in social work, some medical posts, and many management roles too – so discussion skills are vital.

The topic you will be asked to discuss will vary and is likely to become more complex the further up the career ladder you are. At a management development centre you could be asked to join in a discussion concerning a proposed merger with another company, whereas at graduate level a more general topic might be allocated. Generally, even if discussions do involve current affairs topics, you won't be asked to discuss subjects that pry into your personal politics. The following examples are typically what you might expect.

The rescue exercise

There are several versions of one exercise that comes up often at graduate selection. It goes under the name of 'cave rescue', 'moon rescue' or similar. Each candidate is given an identical set of information and allocated some time, say five minutes, to consider it. During this time, candidates are asked not to talk to one another. Below is an example.

Example 8.1

An avalanche has stranded a group of six climbers at the top of a mountain. There had been no avalanche warning, so the group had not come prepared for such bad weather or for a long stay. Some of the party have sustained injuries. A mountain rescue team has set out, but it is only a small team and can only rescue one climber at a time. The weather is forecast to get worse, so there is a possibility that not everyone who is stranded will be rescued before further landslides and severe falls in temperature cut people off and make rescue impossible.

The members of the party are:

- **Roger** is 43 and is married with two children – a son aged 16 and a daughter aged 12. Roger is the leader of the party and the most experienced climber.
- **Harold** is 58 and is the oldest member of the party. He has had some experience of climbing. He used to be a maths and PE teacher, but he took early retirement when he developed heart problems and he has recently had a heart bypass operation. He has been working hard to get fit again and was very keen to complete this climb. The cold is really getting to him and he has not brought his medication with him – he had assumed he would be home by evening.
- **Gillian** is 36 and works as a nurse at the local hospital. She is not married and does not have any children, though she has just started going out with one of the doctors at the hospital. Her elderly mother lives nearby and Gillian helps her mother a great deal with shopping, gardening and other general support.
- **Robert**, aged 17, is the youngest member of the party. He has been in a youth custody centre for several offences of taking and driving away vehicles. Roger, the group leader, met Robert when he was doing some voluntary work at the centre and he encouraged Robert to get involved in activities like climbing to help raise his self-esteem and stay out of trouble. Robert has not managed to find a job yet and he has committed one minor theft since he has been released from custody, but he really wants to stay out of trouble and he has come on the climb to keep out of the way of some of his less desirable acquaintances. His right leg has been badly injured and he has lost a considerable amount of blood.
- **Michelle** is 22 and is coming to the end of her degree in development studies. She is planning to do voluntary work overseas for a year or two once she

has completed her course and one of her reasons for joining this climb is that she feels it will help her confidence and her ability to cope in new and different situations. She has a younger brother and a younger sister, but her father died a year before she was due to start her university course.

■ **Maria** is 51. She is divorced and has four children. Only the youngest son now lives at home with her – he is 10. She works from home, doing mainly bookkeeping, and intends to go back to college, or perhaps do an Open University course when Jack, her son, is settled into secondary school in a year or two's time.

The participants in the discussion are then asked to discuss in which order they feel the six unfortunate individuals should be rescued.

The harsher versions of this exercise make it inevitable that some people will not survive. The issues are always made deliberately difficult in order to create some real grounds for discussion. The group will be asked to achieve consensus if they can and there will be a time limit of 20–30 minutes. At least one observer, usually two, will be listening to the discussion and taking notes of how participants behave, what they contribute and how they react to other members of the group.

Business-related discussions

Topics for discussion may be related more closely to a typical business scenario. For instance, you may be a group of managers who have come together to discuss an issue concerning a particular employee and you are trying to reach a consensus about how to move forward.

Example 8.2

Alan is a software designer who joined your company two years ago. He has a first class degree in information technology with business studies and he spent a sandwich year with one of your most significant competitors as part of his course. He had a number of temporary IT jobs for a year or two before joining you. He had good references, though looking back they tended to stress his technical expertise and problem-solving skills and said very little about his communication skills. He gave a reasonable interview and scored very well on the batch of aptitude tests that he was set, especially the computer aptitude test.

He has turned out to be a mixed blessing. His work in product development has been unquestionably brilliant – he has been the major force behind the design of two new and highly successful products that have made considerable money for your company. On the down side, however, he is extremely difficult to work with. He has upset several members of staff and one reliable technical assistant has already left because he found Alan intolerable. His brilliance is also rather patchy. He will have a good phase where ideas come thick and fast and then will appear uninterested in his work. He has been warned about time keeping, or simply not showing up for work, and he has not taken any notice.

You are a small company, so it is inevitable that most of your staff, even on the technical development side, will come into contact with clients. Alan has been off-hand and quite impatient with clients in the past. You have all reached the stage where a decision has to be made. These are some of the options on the table:

- Ignore the situation – Alan is very good for your company, he has helped you keep a good position in the market place, and if you lose him he will probably go to work for one of your competitors.
- Fire him – there are plenty of bright people around with his skills and you are too busy to spend so much time dealing with one individual and the problems he creates.
- Offer him training in communication skills, time management, etc. and make it clear that if he is not prepared to accept this then you will have to let him go.
- Talk to him about what he finds difficult and whether there are steps he would like to take to improve the situation. Ask him if there is anything that is troubling him.

- Set a clear timetable for some definite improvements, being sure to set specific targets to measure this improvement.
- Other solutions of your own.

A wide range of options is on offer and – as with the avalanche discussion – there is not necessarily a right answer. Your assessors will, once more, be looking for evidence of your ability to think logically, to communicate well and to have some commonsense in your approach to business problems. You are not expected to demonstrate your expertise on employment legislation.

Role play

For many assessed discussion sessions, you are not only asked to discuss the topic in hand, you are also allocated specific roles within this discussion group. For example, you might be told that you are a company director, the chief accountant or a representative from human resources. This gives you two tasks in one, because not only do you have to consider all the points about making a good contribution, you also have to think about the role you are taking. This does not mean that your acting skills are under scrutiny, but it does demand that you think about the business or organizational situation you are in and that you try to contribute appropriately and hold to a certain point of view if you have been asked to do so.

In these situations you will be given written information about the topic that is to be discussed, the background information, and you may be given guidance on the line that you should try to take.

Example 8.3

Swift-Solutions Services was established six years ago. It employs 115 staff and supplies specialist software solutions to a wide range of small businesses. It has been highly successful, building from an initial staff of 11 to its current number. It had been financially successful every year until last year when, although it did not make a loss, it only just broke even. It is by no means a disaster, but external accountants have suggested that it would make sense to apply some cost-cutting measures to turn things around next year and then see where to go next.

You might be allocated one of the following roles:

- **The Company Director.** The company was your brainchild – with a background in IT you put money and commitment into the company and you are really enthusiastic about it. You have heard news that another larger company would like to buy you out and you will fight this determinedly.
- **Head of Finance.** You have been with the company for four years. Eighteen months ago you were advising that although the company was successful the market place was becoming quite crowded and so it might be wise to hold back on recruitment and look at some cost-cutting measures.
- **Head of Marketing.** You joined the company 18 months ago. You led the development of an aggressive marketing strategy, which required considerable financial input. As yet, the benefits have not been fully realized, but you think this is the time for a confident rather than a cautious approach.
- **Head of Human Resources.** You were with the company when it started, although in a different role (as the main Customer Services Manager). You have developed a strong interest in staff training, believing that it pays real dividends – not just in ensuring that your staff works more effectively with customers, but also in aiding staff retention. You see this as an essential part of the company's continued success, not a luxury extra.
- **Deputy Director.** You have been with the company for three years. You have heard that another company might be interested in buying out Swift-Solutions Services. You are not convinced that this is such a bad idea, since you can foresee times getting more difficult for smaller companies like yours. You feel fairly confident that with your own track record you could probably hold on to and develop a place for yourself in the larger company that would emerge. If not, you know that you are highly employable, with innovative product development being one of your main strengths.

This example is just an illustration of what to expect; often there may be more than five participants – between six and ten is common. You would be given additional background papers, so that you had more facts and figures to work with, as well as the information about your 'character'. However, the fact that you are given guidelines about your character's point of view does not mean that you have to remain dogged and inflexible. Other participants may put their point of view persuasively and in the end you have to reach some kind of consensus about how to achieve savings.

Effective participation

If you are asked to participate in discussions like these, be aware that it is not actually your moral principles that are being tested – even though it can feel that way. What are being tested are all the skills and qualities that make for a good communicator. The assessors will want to know if you can:

■ make space to get yourself heard;

■ put your points across clearly;

■ listen to the point of view of others;

■ encourage quieter members of the group to join in;

■ develop an argument and stick to it;

■ be flexible and perhaps alter your point of view if flaws in your argument are pointed out;

■ deal calmly with criticism;

■ criticize others without being offensive;

■ pose questions that make other people think;

■ draw points together at the end of a discussion;

■ summarize arguments;

■ get others to work towards consensus.

There is no one successful model for being good in a discussion, but there are certain guidelines that apply more or less universally. First, never show those tell-tale signs of aggression such as raising your voice, constantly interrupting others before they have finished, or banging on the table, or being rude to other participants. These all show that you can't cope very well in a stressful situation.

Most important of all, never, ever fail to say anything at all. This is difficult if you are a slightly quieter person and you find yourself placed with a group of seemingly confident candidates and are worried about how to get a word in edgeways. But the longer the period of time that passes before you say a word, the more difficult it becomes and the more tense you get. Don't worry too much that your first comment needs to be a really profound and perceptive one, just take a chance so that you can start relating to the rest of the group – you can make more impact as you go along.

There is advice in Chapter 11 (reflecting on tests) on how to develop the ability to be assertive and confident, if this is an area where you feel you could benefit from some further development.

Top tips for making a real contribution to a discussion

- Read any information you are given carefully.

- Think about what you would like to say and how you might introduce your point of view.

- Don't try to rehearse, parrot fashion, comments that you think you would like to make because these will change as the discussion develops.

- Listen to other people, so that what you say is a response not just a statement.

- Encourage participation from any quiet members of the group – this is not pure altruism, it will be observed and approved of by your assessors.

- Don't lose your temper.

- Reflect on your own performance to see what you might do differently if you were in the same situation again.

9 | Discrimination, fair and unfair

In this chapter:

- How different tests are biased

- Let the employer know in advance

- Culture, age and gender bias

- Appropriate tests and conditions

How different tests are biased

Of course all types of selection test do discriminate – this is exactly their purpose. It would not be of any use to an employer to set a test that was so difficult that nobody achieved a reasonable score or passed, or to set something so easy that every applicant passed. Tests are designed to discriminate. However, what they should not do is discriminate unfairly on grounds of age, gender, ethnicity, social background or disability. Anyone using selection tests should take these factors into account in both the administration of the tests and the interpretation of the results. Occupational psychologists and test design and development organizations are certainly aware of these factors and they do take them into account when they are creating tests and establishing the normal range of scores that candidates are expected to achieve.

Of course employers do not set out to deliberately discriminate, not least because of the legal obligations placed upon them to comply with equal opportunities legislation. They also want to recruit the most suitably qualified and capable individuals, so if tests are unfairly biased in some way they may be selecting out some of the very people who would serve the organization well. While legislation only directly affects gender, race and disability, many companies have their own equal opportunities policies that are broader in their scope, including age and socio-economic background. It is also likely that discrimination is an area where legislation will expand; Ireland, for example, already has a policy against discriminating on grounds of age.

Let the employer know in advance

If you have been invited to attend a test session and you do have a disability or any other issue about equal opportunities that concerns you, you should raise this immediately and not wait until you turn up for the test. For example, if you have a visual impairment then tests presented in booklet form or via a computer will pose a problem for you. It is quite possible that the employer will be able to arrange for you to take the test in another format – you may be able to have the questions read out to you and/or dictate your answers, you may be able to have magnification software put on to a computer you will be using, or be given test material in a large print or Braille format. The employer who is testing you will have to get back to the test publishers to discuss what options they can provide and what guidance they can offer, but all this will take extra time.

Only you are aware of the ways in which you can realistically work, so by discussing this in advance the employer has the best possible chance of treating you fairly. Remember that some diagrammatic tests use different colours to distinguish between similar symbols or commands, so if you are colour blind this is also something you need to discuss in advance of your test session. In the same way, if you know you are dyslexic and will face some difficulties with the sorts of tests outlined in this book, the employer may be able to make alternative arrangements for you, such as allowing extra time or providing a scribe. Again, the employer is likely to need to talk to whoever created the test to ensure that they are giving you appropriate help without giving you an advantage over the other candidates.

Visual impairment and dyslexia are obvious examples to pick because there are clear reasons why test material formats and methods of providing your answers can prevent problems. You may have other disabilities, such as a hearing impairment, that you may not think give you any difficulty, but remember that there are often verbal as well as written instructions given at the start of a test. This could also be relevant if you have been asked to join in discussion or presentation sessions where you require feedback from your audience.

It is also important that you are tested for what the test is designed to measure. For example, you may have some motor difficulty, or RSI, which means it is difficult for you to write quickly. In a test of numerical reasoning you do not want to achieve a low score just because you were unable to cope with writing the answers – your score should reflect your ability with numbers and numerical data.

In any of these instances only you know how you have dealt with academic examinations, work situations, professional assessments, etc. in the past, so you are in the best position to guide an employer or a psychologist.

Since the Disability Discrimination Act came into being, employers have been alert to their responsibility for treating people fairly in the selection process, but there are still instances where they are dealing with a particular circumstance for the first time, so they need to know what arrangements to make.

Culture, age and gender bias

Certainly the major testing companies which operate within the graduate market place are aware of the nature of the graduate population and they do work hard to develop appropriate questions and appropriate scoring systems to try to avoid cultural bias. Of course, there is an issue for any applicant whose first language is not English. Completing verbal reasoning tests in a language with which you are not totally fluent and comfortable is difficult. Indeed, completing numerical reasoning tests in these circumstances is also hard because different languages may express mathematical concepts in different ways.

Some tests are published in several languages and you may have the option of asking an employer if they can allow you to do the test in another language. However, this is not necessarily a good move. If you are applying to work for an organization whose main language is English, then the chances are that you are not doing yourself any favours by asking to take the test in another language. The only exception to this could be where a company is advertising posts or has significant operations in countries where the first language is your first language. Then your language becomes a possible personal selling point and you are likely to have mentioned it on your application form or CV.

There are some factors relating to age and gender that remain constant in the testing process. You often hear the comment from people that they don't think as quickly as they used to and there is probably some truth in what they say. On many aptitude and ability tests the highest scores appear to be obtained from those in their mid-teens to late twenties, with a gradual decline after this. Of course, there are also many factors that will work the other way for the older applicant. They have had more work experience, they have learned to use their personality and the skills and qualities they do possess more effectively in the work environment and their knowledge of their own work sector will be far greater than someone who is new to this field.

A consistent picture also emerges of some gender differences in aptitude tests. On the whole, males obtain higher scores in diagrammatic and spatial reasoning, while females do better in verbal reasoning and speed and accuracy tests. These factors should all be accounted for properly if the test has been well designed and if those who administer and interpret results are suitably qualified to do so.

Appropriate tests and conditions

As you climb the ladder in your chosen career, the tests you face are more likely to be set on an individual basis by a company psychologist or a recruitment consultant. This means that while the test will still be administered in the strict conditions appropriate to a particular test, you are more likely to meet the person who is going to test you some time before the test session for an initial interview. You can therefore raise any concerns you have.

Unfortunately, recruitment consultants and headhunters may not always have the same back-up as someone in the human resource department of a multinational company. If you do have concerns about the competence or behaviour of the person who tested you, or the relevance and validity of the tests you were asked to take, the British Psychological Society Testing Centre provides valuable information. Comprehensive reviews of personality and aptitude tests that they produce are now available through their website and their directories are also available from some reference and university libraries. The British Psychological Society produces a code of practice for occupational testing and guidelines for test users and test takers and these can also be accessed through their website. Everyone who administers and interprets aptitude tests should have a list B certificate, while for personality tests, because the interpretation and feedback is more complicated, they should be qualified to level A certificate standard. In addition, test publishers run training courses to allow appropriately qualified individuals to administer specific aptitude and personality tests.

With the changing nature of the graduate population, the more global nature of many large businesses and individuals facing the prospect of several job changes throughout their working lives, many test developers and publishers are now paying more attention to the issue of giving all candidates the same chances of success. The ABLE series published by the Oxford Psychologists Press (OPP) (mentioned briefly in Chapter 2) is a case in point. These tests are not like the traditional aptitude test batteries with separate tests for verbal reasoning, numerical reasoning and diagrammatic reasoning, or whatever combination an employer chooses to use. They are a series of business learning exercises where candidates are asked to sort through a range of materials rather like in-tray exercises. Candidates are given sets of information – correspondence, numerical data, brief reports, etc. – and are asked to work out solutions to particular problems by referring to this material. The tests are built around specific business issues, for example financial appraisal, vetting applications, interpreting legal information and critical information analysis.

OPP has carried out an analysis of both male and female scores and majority and minority groups within a culture and has had encouraging results. To understand the fairness of a psychometric test it is necessary to monitor how different social groups perform in it. If one group tends to achieve higher scores than another, then the test is said to have adverse impact with respect to the group which scores less well. In a perfect world tests have adverse impact scores of zero, so occupational psychologists and test designers seek the lowest possible adverse impact scores with every test they develop. Research on the ABLE series shows that these tests are achieving a very low adverse impact in both gender comparisons and majority/minority population groups. This does not imply that other tests are not good or not fair, or that all test designers are not working hard to make their tests as fair as possible. However, it is an interesting example of an initiative that appears to be a response to the very particular needs of the current UK employment market.

Making a complaint

If you do feel that for any reason you have been discriminated against unfairly during the test-taking process and you want to follow this up, there are steps you can take. Part 3 of this book focuses on sources of further advice and information and gives contact details for the Equal Opportunities Commission, the Commission for Racial Equality and further information on the Disability Rights Commission.

It is also clear that organizations that design tests do not want their materials to be used unfairly and inappropriately – when researching for this book several companies made this point strongly to me. If you know which company designed the test – and this information is normally clearly visible on the test booklet or computer screen – then you can get back to them and raise your concern. They are not in a position to take up your individual case, but if they do receive feedback that a particular employer or recruitment consultant is using their materials in a way that they deem inappropriate, they are able to follow it up from that angle.

Complaints about discrimination in the testing process are rare. Companies with considerable experience of recruitment and recruitment issues – many of which have clearly stated equal opportunities policies, to which they are committed – use tests. Taking action is always a difficult and very personal decision because you have to weigh up the cost to yourself in terms of time and stress and what you are likely to gain from it.

10 Are you write for the job?

In this chapter:

- Graphology in recruitment

- Graphology in action

Graphology in recruitment

Graphology is an interpretation of someone's personality, temperament, strengths and weaknesses via the analysis of a piece of their handwriting. The theory behind it is that the individual's handwriting, however they are taught, will gradually flow into a personal style that expresses the individuality of their brain.

While many psychologists and recruiters are highly sceptical of such a selection tool and express concern that it does not constitute an objective measure of personality or aptitude, the fact remains that there are employers who choose to use it. In some countries it is very popular and it would be quite routine for job applicants to be asked to submit a sample of their handwriting for analysis. France is probably the leader in applying this method of selection, but Germany, Israel, Switzerland, the USA and to some extent the UK also have companies which choose to use graphology as part of their selection procedure.

Graphologists say that the analysis they produce can be as revealing as any personality questionnaire or interview, highlighting a whole range of personal characteristics that would interest employers. Creativity, imagination, ambition, conformity, risk taking, team spirit, energy levels and self-confidence are just some of the traits and qualities that an analysis would reveal. Weaknesses, such as inability to cope with pressure, impatience and lack of confidence, are some of the negative areas that can be revealed.

What to expect

The emphasis in this book is to look at how candidates can prepare for and plan to do better at selection 'tests', but in the case of handwriting analysis there is little to be done in terms of preparation. The advice that practising graphologists do give to candidates is simply to write as naturally as you can – just as you would write a note to a colleague or a letter to a friend. This is quite important advice, because there is usually an understandable inclination to try to make your writing look neater if you know that it is to be analyzed. In fact, this may be entirely the wrong thing to do – neat handwriting may, for example, suggest an over controlling and obsessive nature.

Graphologists analyze many aspects of writing – its size, the direction in which it slopes, the straightness of lines on the page, how 't's are crossed or 'i's dotted, roundness of loops, unfinished letters, etc. There are no obvious ways to 'improve' your writing to produce a different personality profile.

You should always be told if your handwriting is going to be subjected to analysis. If you are asked to accompany your CV with a handwritten covering letter, the chances are that this is not because it will be analyzed – it is to see whether you have legible handwriting. The tendency to require handwritten covering letters is, in any case, on the decline. Graphologists who belong to the British Institute of Graphologists have a code of practice that says someone should always be told if their handwriting is to be used as part of the recruitment process. The only exception to this is that occasionally the writing of a current employee may be submitted for analysis by a manager who has concerns about that person and wants more information before they decide how to act.

Graphology in action

Human resource managers who have used graphology as part of their selection procedures or ongoing career development exercises do feel that it yields worthwhile results. In some cases it appears to confirm the results of the selection interview, but on some occasions a handwriting analysis reveals a cause for concern that had not come to light in the interview. I spoke to one human resource manager who told me that a handwriting analysis of a candidate had indicated a significant lack of confidence and yet in the interview he had come across as self-assured and able to cope. She had employed him, but he had in fact left the company, because of a lack of confidence in the way he managed staff in his team. One human resource manager also told me that she had found it particularly useful in recruiting some engineering and technical staff, where she felt the handwriting analysis had revealed more than the interview. There are undoubtedly instances – though rare – of candidates who have done very well in all aspects of the selection process and then found a company dubious about employing them because of what a handwriting analysis has revealed.

However, graphology is something that employers taking on large numbers of graduates or going for any other major recruitment drives are not likely to use. Unlike many of the other tests described in this book, where marking is more standardized or can be done by computer, a graphologist has to make individual analyses and this is a costly process for the employer. Therefore it may be the company recruiting the one-off manager or professional which is more likely to use this technique. In the UK there does not appear to be a pattern of particular sizes or types of employer that have developed an enthusiasm for this recruitment method.

The fact remains that however dubious a candidate may feel about such a technique, if it is one that your prospective employer chooses to apply, then you will have to be prepared for it.

Top tips for dealing with handwriting analyses

- If you are asked to submit a handwriting sample and not told why, then don't be afraid to ask.

- Write as you would normally – don't be obsessed with trying to portray a neat and tidy personality.

- Be aware that in today's more global employment market you will have to face whatever selection tests are prevalent and popular with different organizations in different regions of the world.

- It is unlikely that a handwriting analysis will be the single selection tool used by an employer, so don't worry about it too much.

- If you do want to have your handwriting analyzed to check what sort of profile is produced, then to do this privately will cost you about £60.00 for a one-hour session. You should check what you would be charged before booking a session, just as you would for any other service. Details of the British Institute of Graphologists are listed in the sources of information at the end of this book.

11 Reflecting on tests

In this chapter:

- Self-assessment

- Using feedback

- Aim to do better

- Possibilities for change

One of the most frustrating issues, from a candidate's point of view, is that often the results of aptitude tests will not be given back to you. Obviously the employer is obliged to treat results responsibly, but giving test information back is time consuming. Often the only way that you know whether you did well or not is by whether you are offered the job or move on to the next stage of selection. Individual recruitment consultants, who either administer tests or employ occupational psychologists to do so, may be more able to give you feedback on your results, but otherwise you are left somewhat in the dark.

Furthermore, your own subjective reactions as to how you did are not always accurate. Many graduates will emerge from test sessions feeling rather despondent; a reaction shared by senior management staff who have been put through a gruelling promotion selection. This does not necessarily mean you have done badly. You will undoubtedly feel tired and you may have tackled questions and exercises on which you find it hard to assess your own performance. A common reaction from candidates is that they expect to do well on verbal tests and often feel a bit put out if these seemed difficult.

Self-assessment

It is worth attempting an assessment of some aspects of your performance yourself.

The point of this self-assessment is neither to give yourself a pat on the back nor to give yourself a hard time, but to give you some clear ideas about where you need to put in work for future assessments.

Post-test checklist

Verbal reasoning tests	I found many words I did not understand	Yes/No
	I found the written passages confusing	Yes/No
	I found the questions difficult to answer	Yes/No
	I found it got harder as it went along	Yes/No
	I found I was pushed for time	Yes/No
	I really enjoyed the whole test	Yes/No
	It was different to anything I have seen before	Yes/No
Numerical reasoning tests	Some of the charts and diagrams looked unfamiliar	Yes/No
	I found interpreting the data difficult	Yes/No
	I did not understand some of the mathematical symbols	Yes/No
	I had forgotten how to use a calculator	Yes/No
	I found it hard to complete all the questions – I could have completed them if I had had more time	Yes/No

	I found the questions fairly easy	Yes/No
	I enjoy working with numbers	Yes/No
Diagrammatical reasoning tests	The diagrams were different to anything I have seen before	Yes/No
	I found it quite difficult to understand the diagrams	Yes/No
	I found the questions difficult to answer	Yes/No
	I found it difficult to answer all the questions in the time allowed	Yes/No
Business exercises	I found it difficult to deal with so much paperwork	Yes/No
	I found it hard to know what was expected of me	Yes/No
	I found it difficult to decide which information was relevant	Yes/No
	I did not feel confident about the decisions I was taking	Yes/No
	I found I had not organized my time very effectively	Yes/No
	I really enjoyed the exercises – it was good working on 'real' problems	Yes/No
	It was easy to work within the time limit	Yes/No
Giving a presentation	I was quite nervous	Yes/No
	I had prepared too much material	Yes/No
	I think the audience could hear me easily	Yes/No
	My presentation had a good structure with a clear beginning and a summary and conclusion	Yes/No
	I ran out of material	Yes/No
	I ran over time, or had to leave important things out	Yes/No

	I believe the audience enjoyed it and felt involved	Yes/No
	I really enjoyed myself – I felt confident and in control	Yes/No
Participating in a discussion	It was a while before I felt comfortable joining in	Yes/No
	I was thinking so hard about what to say, I tended to miss out on what other people were saying	Yes/No
	I found it easy to say what I wanted to	Yes/No
	I felt people were paying attention to what I was saying	Yes/No
	I got a bit irritated and let it show	Yes/No
	I encouraged quieter participants to join in	Yes/No
	I found the whole experience rather stressful – I was glad when it was over	Yes/No
	It was enjoyable and I felt quite comfortable	Yes/No
Personality questionnaires	I felt uncomfortable answering some of the questions	Yes/No
	It was interesting and enjoyable	Yes/No

Using feedback

If you are fortunate enough to gain some feedback from your test sessions, try to make use of it. If you took a battery of tests it is helpful to know if you scored well or poorly against other candidates in the different types of test you took. If, for example, it emerges that you are weak on numerical tests but strong on verbal tests, revisit Chapter 3 on preparation for tests and look at some of the steps you can take to improve your performance.

The results of personality questionnaires are more complex to interpret and more time is needed to give these back to candidates. There are no right or wrong answers and there are no necessarily good or bad scores. In occupational settings, employers will have profiles of the sort of people they require for particular jobs and the point of the questionnaire results is to see how well candidates match up to these profiles. The company is likely to have a range of ideal profile matches for different jobs on offer. If you are given some feedback, you may learn, for example, that you are likely to work more effectively if you have a lot of autonomy, if you have a clear structure to work to, if you have a lot of contact with other colleagues, if you are given responsibility – the possibilities are many and varied. The point is that such a result is not saying you are a success or a failure, but rather that you work better in some situations than others and those situations align better with some jobs than others.

Don't be discouraged

Remember that tests form only part of the selection procedure. At selection and development centres you will have taken part in a range of different methods of selection and you probably found some exercises easier than others. It is likely that at a selection centre those assessing you are looking for a range of different results, according to the job for which you are applying. Several large organizations recruit graduates from one battery of tests for many different departments. For example, they might recruit some into project management, some into engineering, others into marketing, etc. They may well be looking for different sets of scores across those different disciplines to match the different job profiles that they have drawn up for the various work areas they have on offer. IT specialists, for example, might be expected to achieve a higher score in the diagrammatic reasoning test in order to be successful, whilst someone going into marketing would be expected to score well on anything that assesses communication (personality profiles, group presentation exercises and verbal reasoning tests).

If you are certain that you do have consistently weak areas, you might worry whether this is an indication that you are looking for the wrong sort of job and whether this weakness will always be a hurdle. Don't overreact and decide, on the strength of one or even a few negative test results, that you must completely rethink your career plan and seek a change of direction. If you are performing poorly on tests and exercises that will form a core of the job however, perhaps you do need to ask whether you would really be happy and successful in that job or profession. Sometimes, for example, applicants may not realize how much of the work of an accountant is about dealing with words and people rather than numbers, or how great a level of computer aptitude is required for some jobs that look as if they are more about writing skills.

Aim to do better

Before rethinking your next job application or changing your career direction, consider the ways in which you can aim to do better the next time you take any form of selection test.

Weak spots with words

Revisit the suggestions in Chapter 3 on improving your verbal skills. If you are a university student your university may offer study skills in English and English usage. If you are currently employed with a large organization, its training section may offer courses on such topics as report writing or minute taking. You might also find that courses offered by your local adult education institute are relevant. What is on offer varies from area to area, but business communications and creative writing are topics that you might consider.

The most important thing is to do something enjoyable as well as useful. You can't gear your whole life towards finding ways of doing better at selection tests. It is far better to do things that equip you with skills and knowledge that improve your day-to-day performance at work or in your studies – and hopefully increase your job satisfaction and your self-confidence too.

Nasty numbers

There are many people who didn't really enjoy maths at school, have had little to do with it since and have developed if not a phobia then a definite anxiety about dealing with numbers. The fact that you were not brilliant at trigonometry or quadratic equations does not mean that you necessarily lack the number skills to check a balance sheet, look over a department's budget or estimate the profitability of a particular venture. Returning to maths with an open mind will really help.

It is always possible to join an evening class in maths, pay for some private tuition if you can afford it and feel it is worth it or, if you are a university student, see what study skills options are on offer at your university – many offer maths teaching as part of a study skills or study support programme.

Remember that some of the highest salaries are paid to people with good numerical skills, such as accountants, actuaries and those who work on the financial aspects of management consultancy – a good incentive to improve your numerical skills!

Disastrous diagrams

It is less easy to find obvious ways to improve your performance on diagrammatic reasoning tests. They are popular precisely because they are not language dependent, but appear to correlate with a more general measure of intelligence. However, many 'Test Your Own IQ' books and puzzle books contain examples of these exercises, so by going through practice material you can start to train yourself to think in particular ways. Some people appear to think in this style quite naturally – you can spot them expressing ideas and plans in the form of diagrams rather than lists of words – so if you can find anyone like this it is not a bad idea to team up with them and get them to explain how they visualize problems or ideas.

Use every practice opportunity

If you possibly can, find opportunities to take aptitude tests before you have to do these as part of your search for a job. Again, university students are in a good position because most university careers services offer the chance to sit practice tests that are designed by the same companies that work with employers. These tests are offered in strict test conditions, but the real plus for them is that you are able to discuss your result in detail with careers advisers. They will be able to tell you whether you performed differently on different tests such as verbal, numerical and diagrammatic reasoning. They will not be able to say that you would or would not be successful if you were tested by such and such a company, but they will be able to rate your performance against norm groups measured from the whole graduate population. Most university careers services extend this option to take tests to students who have graduated in the past two years, though some may make a charge for this service.

If you are not a current or recent student, it is not quite so easy to take practice tests. However, many independent careers consultants and occupational psychologists can offer you this option, as long as they are qualified as testers. The companies which supply tests will not supply them to people who have not been trained both to administer the tests and interpret the results.

It is also worth looking at the websites of the major test publishers (listed in Part 3), since some of these do contain practice material.

Plenty of personality

If there is general agreement that personality is based on a combination of innate factors and learning, then a person is unlikely to undergo a complete change and personality tests are not designed to suggest that they should. Understanding more about the way you behave and react to situations at work, though, can give you an opportunity to learn and develop. We do learn from experience and most people are able to look back on work or study situations and feel that we would handle them differently with the greater insight we now have about our own behaviour and the workings of organizations. Remember that one of the dimensions in the Emotional Intelligence Quota is a measure of how we can adapt our behaviour and learn new ways to deal with changing situations.

Possibilities for change

You may have discovered through personality questionnaire profiles or through your performance in a selection exercise (such as giving a presentation, joining in a discussion or solving a business problem) that there are some aspects of your behaviour that you would like to develop, alter or control. These are not likely to be aspects that come as an enormous shock to you because they are likely to be reflected in how you deal with situations in your life at work and elsewhere.

While personality is in some ways constant – otherwise personality measures would be pointless – there is no doubt that it is possible to develop more effective ways of dealing with situations, to be aware of areas where you need to look at new ways of working and also to be aware of your strengths and enhance them. The exercises and tests discussed in this book tap into many aspects of personality and behaviour and the following sections give some ideas of ways to tackle some of the most common causes of concern. But before you plan ways to change your behaviour you do need to ask yourself a few questions:

- What is the problem I have – for example, is it lack of confidence, disorganized work style, anxiety about taking decisions?

- What areas of my working life does it affect?

- Is it a problem that affects me a lot (most working days and most projects) or only occasionally?

- What can I do about it?

Two examples of behaviour styles that may adversely affect your working life are often picked up in various selection and test situations: lack of assertiveness and poor planning.

Learning to be more assertive

Over the last 20 years 'assertiveness' is a word that has appeared more and more in job advertisements, job descriptions and as a part of many staff development programmes, training courses and classes. This is no passing fad, but a key competence for dealing with many work situations and also for giving individuals a model for behaviour that has helped many people to operate more successfully and feel much more at ease.

Assertiveness is the ability to tread that useful middle path between being an aggressive bully and a complete pushover (referred to as passive). Of course, most people do not operate at those extremes, but many people do feel they are further from that ideal midpoint than they would choose to be.

If your behaviour is too passive you are likely to put other people's needs – their requests for tasks to be completed, their standpoint in an argument, etc. – before your own. This can mean that you find it hard to defend an idea or a proposal, even if it makes good sense, because others can easily shout you down. It can mean that your work becomes disorganized because you are constantly responding to the demands of others, rather than working out what you ought to do first in order to achieve success. The chances are that you also feel irritated with yourself because you don't want to respond in this way. Consider how you behaved in discussion exercises, in responding to questions when you gave a presentation or in how you looked at selecting priorities in a business exercise and ask yourself whether you behaved in a typically passive way.

Aggressive behaviour is the polar opposite and is typified by satisfying your own needs, putting demands on others, not listening to someone else's point of view and possibly losing sight of the wider goals of a team or a project. Not only is this difficult for others to deal with, but it is often a cover-up for feeling insecure or inadequate, and feeling anxious about your work performance and whether you are really going to achieve what you would like to. You may have seen elements of this in your own performance either in test situations or in real work situations.

Most of us have observed instances of both over-passive and over-aggressive behaviour in colleagues, so we should know the tell-tale signs. Having elements of both these qualities is not all bad – passive people can be considerate colleagues and aggressive people often put a great deal of energy into their work. Assertive behaviour, however, can allow you to get the best of both worlds. Assertive people are concerned with their own opinions, but equally with the opinions, ideas and feelings of others and the assertive worker tries to achieve win-win situations.

Becoming more assertive is not simply about becoming a more pleasant person to work with, but because it involves having respect for your own views and those of others it tends automatically to engender respect from others. If you have a good project idea, or an imaginative idea for solving a problem, you are far more likely to be listened to. Being more assertive also has knock-on effects on many characteristics sought by employers. It is easier to be more persuasive and to influence other people and it can improve self-confidence significantly.

Assertive behaviour is something that can undoubtedly be developed and practised by employing some quite simple techniques.

Top tips **for assertive behaviour**

- Use more statements beginning with 'I'. For example, say 'I believe we should', 'I think a way to tackle this would be', 'I feel concerned about this' rather than 'Perhaps it would be possible' – in this instance you are not really owning what you think or believe.

- Try not to use qualifying statements like 'I wonder whether you could'. Instead say 'Please can you' – in this way you are showing respect while making it clear what you want.

- Ask other people for their opinions, for example 'What do you think we should do?'.

Learning to be a more effective planner

If you have found in-tray exercises difficult or you know that planning effectively is one of your weaker areas, this is something you can work to change. How often do you see a job advertisement that asks if you are good at meeting deadlines, or an application form that requires you to outline how you go about planning a project? How truthful are your answers?

Disorganization may be one aspect of the highly creative individual, but it is hard work for colleagues and hard work for the person concerned. Even if you can usually scrape by while leaving things until the last minute, it is not desirable in a busy commercial or professional environment.

Planning involves first defining a goal you wish to achieve and second working out what steps you will take to achieve it. A good goal should be realistic with a measurable outcome and a defined timescale. Anyone who has been involved in putting in bids for funding or tenders for contracts will be familiar with this process on paper, and your own work planning should mirror this type of process. It sounds obvious, but a sensible starting point is to keep a diary and use it – not just to remind yourself of dates of meetings or deadlines, but to outline the different tasks and processes you need to go through to plan for that meeting or complete that assignment. If the 'One of those days' exercise in Chapter 7 struck a chord, then this advice is undoubtedly apt for you.

Without becoming one of those people who makes endless lists and then divides them into further lists – so that your main pre-occupation becomes list writing rather than completing the tasks – a written structure will help you. It also gives you a way of measuring your progress and gives you a sense of achievement. This may not be as easy as it sounds. Depending on what kind of person you are, you may feel that this approach will stifle your creativity and that the structures you impose upon yourself will mean that you don't produce such a good piece of work in the end.

You might have to ease yourself into this way of working in small stages and also give yourself permission to make some alterations to your plans and build in the option for flexibility. Anticipate likely problem areas, so that you can begin work on these in plenty of time, and try to involve others in your ideas at an early stage and get support before you embark on anything new.

It is also far easier to delegate effectively if you plan. Delegation is not the art of rushing round at the last minute to see whom you can possibly bully, cajole or bribe into helping you out. It is deciding at the outset of a project or task which colleagues might be assigned various sub-tasks. These tasks may include providing data, researching information, contacting other relevant individuals or giving input with comments and suggestions at various stages throughout the process.

One likely benefit of this approach is that you suffer far less stress in your work situations and that you become a better colleague who gains more respect from peers. You will also find that you are far more likely to get an enthusiastic response to your ideas from colleagues if you have learned to estimate realistic timescales, anticipate objections and explain your thinking fully, rather than admitting that you haven't quite worked it out yet, but you are sure you will get there in the end. Financial as well as human resource support will also be easier to obtain.

Improving your chances of success

These examples of becoming more assertive or developing better planning skills are just two instances where you can look at your behaviour and analyze whether there are situations where you feel you could be more effective and also happier. You can easily extend this to other areas, such as finding ways to feel less stressed, learning ways of presenting more effectively or working to be more open in your dealings with colleagues, clients and customers.

One of the keys to developing new behaviours is to practise them. If you have decided that you are going to be more assertive and less passive in a work situation, choose situations where you can try this out. Above all, choose easy and safe situations first. It is not a good idea to launch the new, more assertive you at a large and important meeting, or use your manager as your first 'guinea-pig'. They may be taken by surprise, but you will also feel more anxious about the situation and the possible outcome. It is also very important to get feedback on your behaviour. Don't just assume that people are reacting in a certain way

– ask them. Try out your new techniques with colleagues with whom you feel comfortable and ask for feedback. Practising new skills and developing your weaker attributes will always help because it will improve your self-knowledge and your confidence.

If all else fails, take heart from a few final thoughts. In the 1980s, when employers found they required increased numbers of recruits with suitable abilities to learn computer programming and systems analysis, they used computer aptitude tests as their main selection tool. Several companies found that they had recruited people who were extremely effective in these fields of information technology, but who were not very successful in team working, dealing with clients or taking on other management tasks. This is not to suggest that people who were good with computers were not good with people, but that the companies had perhaps erred in emphasizing one area of ability over and above all others.

In contrast, some people have skills that would not score highly in any sort of test, and yet they have had successful careers. Sir Peter Parker, who has chaired more than one large corporation, said that he often used to take a 20-minute sleep in the office and woe betide anyone who came near his office during that time. Unconventional methods can lead to success.

The serious point is that aptitude and personality testing is not going to go away. With businesses and other organizations having to cope with changing markets, different skills gaps and a less static workforce, anything that helps them to select, train and keep the best staff is going to remain a constant part of the recruitment process.

part two

practice
material

Verbal tests
Logic tests
Numerical tests
David Singmaster's problems
Saville and Holdsworth tests
Work style questionnaire

Practice material

Verbal tests

Note that in these verbal tests there are no words that have different UK and US spellings, since this would add to the confusion. However, you do need to bear the differences in mind if you are taking an entrance test for a US college or business, or if you end up working for a company that has adopted US spelling.

Spelling

There are hundreds of thousands of words that could be put into a spelling test, but the samples below are words that you are more likely to use or encounter in work and business settings.

Verbal test 1

Look at the following two columns of words and underline any that you think are spelt incorrectly.

1	conglomerate	conglomorate
2	syndicate	syndecate
3	deliberate	deliberate
4	diligent	diligant
5	influenccial	influential
6	solusion	solution

7	accommodation	accomodation
8	contrervene	contravene
9	developement	development
10	disserning	discerning
11	maintenance	maintanance
12	improvment	improvement
13	constitutents	constituents
14	controvercy	controversy
15	serendipity	serrendipity
16	exclussive	exclusive
17	affluant	affluent
18	confidential	confidencial
19	concurring	concuring
20	alternative	alternitive
21	flambouyant	flamboyant
22	aquisitive	acquisitive
23	semantics	cemantics
24	discovery	descovery
25	acceptible	acceptable

Answers

Correct spellings are:

1 conglomerate

2 syndicate

3 deliberate

4 diligent

5 influential

6 solution

7 accommodation

8 contravene

9 development

10 discerning

11 maintenance

12 improvement

13 constituents

14 controversy

15 serendipity

16 exclusive

17 affluent

18 confidential

19 concurring

20 alternative

21 flamboyant

22 acquisitive

23 semantics

24 discovery

25 acceptable

Verbal test 2

Underline any of the following words that are spelt incorrectly.

1 committee

2 legislation

3 senario

4 distributors

5 guarantee

6 corrolory

7 eligible

8 referrals

9 intigrated

10 fallacy

11 warantee

12 legitimate

13 foriegn

14 systematic

15 stattutory

16 credencials

17 contemporary

18 analisys

19 competitors

20 flagreant

Answers

Incorrectly spelt words are:

3 scenario

6 corollary

9 integrated

11 warrantee

13 foreign

15 statutory

16 credentials

18 analysis

20 flagrant

Word placement

Verbal test 3

1 Place the words 'here' and 'hear':

Have you been waiting ... for long?

When did you ... about this afternoon's meeting?

2 Place the words 'site', 'sight' and 'cite':

Have you visited the ... that we intend to develop?

We can ... several documents that indicate our intentions.

Well, the director wearing fancy dress will be an interesting ...

3 Place the words 'breaks' and 'brakes':

I am concerned about how many ... some staff seem to be taking before lunch.

Someone is going to have to put the ... on this before it gets out of hand.

4 Place the words 'stationary' and 'stationery':

How long is it since anyone tidied out the ... cupboard?

I think we are just going to have to remain ... for the time being.

5 Place the words 'fare' and 'fair':

We have to ensure that this new policy is ... to all staff.

I wasn't very impressed with the ... at the launch.

6 Place the words 'too' and 'two':

It is all ... easy to jump to conclusions here.

We need to finish the proposal within the next ... weeks.

7 Place the words 'wait' and 'weight':

We don't want customers to ... any longer than is absolutely necessary.

It is very important that the correct ... is given on every occasion.

8 Place the words 'affect' and 'effect':

This could have quite a significant ... on staff morale.

This is likely to ... the way we develop the latest range of products.

9 Place the words 'principle' and 'principal':

The ... reason for developing the appraisal system is to implement better training policies.

I believe we should stick firmly to our basic ... here – the customer is always right.

10 Place the words 'its' and 'it's':

I wonder if ... always as difficult as this to raise extra income.

Well, the new model gets ... first showing at next month's exhibition.

Answers

1 Have you been waiting here for long?

When did you hear about this afternoon's meeting?

2 Have you visited the site that we intend to develop?

We can cite several documents that indicate our intentions.

Well, the director wearing fancy dress will be an interesting sight.

3 I am concerned about how many breaks some staff seem to be taking before lunch.

Someone is going to have to put the brakes on this before it gets out of hand.

4 How long is it since anyone tidied out the stationery cupboard?

I think we are just going to have to remain stationary for the time being.

5 We have to ensure that this new policy is fair to all staff.

I wasn't very impressed with the fare at the launch.

6 It is all too easy to jump to conclusions here.

We need to finish the proposal within the next two weeks.

7 We don't want customers to wait any longer than is absolutely necessary.

It is very important that the correct weight is given on every occasion.

8 This could have quite a significant effect on staff morale.

This is likely to affect the way we develop the latest range of products.

9 The principal reason for developing the appraisal system is to develop better training policies.

I believe we should stick firmly to our basic principle here – the customer is always right.

10 I wonder if it's always as difficult as this to raise extra income.

Well, the new model gets its first showing at next month's exhibition.

Word relationships

Verbal test 4

1 Man is to boy as woman is to:

(a) daughter   (b) female   (c) girl   (d) lady

2 Food is to eat as water is to:

(a) thirst   (b) drink   (c) bathe   (d) swallow

3 Bird is to nest as man is to:

   (a) house   (b) home   (c) garden   (d) dwelling

4 Bicycle is to car as glider is to:

   (a) aeroplane   (b) sky   (c) fly   (d) parachute

5 Ship is to sea as train is to:

   (a) platform   (b) journey   (c) rail   (d) station

6 Wheel is to turn as flame is to:

   (a) glow   (b) hot   (c) fire   (d) burn

7 Water is to steam as ice is to:

   (a) snow   (b) water   (c) vapour   (d) cold

8 She is to hers as he is to:

   (a) his   (b) him   (c) he's   (d) their

9 Cotton is to thread as copper is to:

   (a) insulation   (b) link   (c) electricity   (d) wire

10 Tree is to forest as pebble is to:

   (a) sand   (b) beach   (c) rock   (d) flint

11 Bank is to money as library is to:

   (a) reader   (b) book   (c) catalogue   (d) reference

12 Black is to white as light is to:

   (a) bulb   (b) glow   (c) dark   (d) bright

13 Grass is to green as sky is to:

   (a) clear   (b) pleasant   (c) blue   (d) cloud

14 Touch is to feel as look is to:

(a) eye   (b) sight   (c) view   (d) see

15 Circle is to sphere as square is to:

(a) oblong   (b) box   (c) cube   (d) ellipse

Answers

1 c

2 b

3 a

4 a

5 c

6 d

7 b

8 a

9 d

10 b

11 b

12 c

13 c

14 d

15 c

Synonyms

Synonyms are words with the same meaning. You need to find a word with a similar meaning from the options provided.

Verbal test 5

1 Lively means the same as:

   (a) energetic   (b) hurried   (c) lethargic   (d) speedy

2 Famous means the same as:

   (a) notorious   (b) celebrity   (c) important   (d) well known

3 Lucid means the same as:

   (a) watery   (b) clear   (c) bright   (d) luminous

4 Intrepid means the same as:

   (a) afraid   (b) sensible   (c) bold   (d) determined

5 Calm means the same as:

   (a) restive   (b) relaxed   (c) slow   (d) apathetic

6 Delve means the same as:

   (a) dig   (b) deep   (c) burrow   (d) bury

7 Furtive means the same as:

   (a) quiet   (b) secretive   (c) whisper   (d) deceptive

8 Concur means the same as:

   (a) dispute   (b) concord   (c) agree   (d) comply

9 Saturnine means the same as:

   (a) silent   (b) sensitive   (c) serious   (d) dejected

10 Passive means the same as:

    (a) tranquil   (b) submissive   (c) easy   (d) gentle

Answers

1 a

2 d

3 b

4 c

5 b

6 a

7 b

8 c

9 d

10 b

Antonyms

Antonyms are words with opposite meanings.

Verbal test 6

1 Prompt is the opposite of:

    (a) swift   (b) hurried   (c) slow   (d) early

2 Accept is the opposite of:

    (a) reject   (b) comply   (c) decide   (d) receive

3 Above is the opposite of:

    (a) under   (b) beneath   (c) beside   (d) nadir

4 Reveal is the opposite of:

(a) expose   (b) relieve   (c) conceal   (d) delete

5 Abbreviate is the opposite of:

(a) extenuate   (b) shorten   (c) lengthen   (d) précis

6 Blunt is the opposite of:

(a) outspoken   (b) flat   (c) hard   (d) sharp

7 Extravagant is the opposite of:

(a) mean   (b) frivolous   (c) cautious   (d) thrifty

8 Restrain is the opposite of:

(a) liberate   (b) constrain   (c) control   (d) reveal

9 Trivial is the opposite of:

(a) crucial   (b) decisive   (c) important   (d) inconsequential

10 Irritating is the opposite of:

(a) soft   (b) soothing   (c) sensitive   (d) sympathetic

Answers

1	c	**6**	d
2	a	**7**	d
3	b	**8**	a
4	c	**9**	c
5	c	**10**	b

When you are completing tests like the last two, you will often find a variety of types of question in the same test. Remember to remain alert to changes from same to opposite – beware of just slipping into a standard pattern to produce your answers.

Logic tests

Logic test 1

1   Susan and Diane like pizza, but Geoff and Chris like pasta. Susan and Geoff both like pasta. Who likes pizza and pasta?

(a) Susan   (b) Diane   (c) Geoff   (d) Chris

2   Joan and Rob earn more than Ian. Michael earns less than Ian. Andrew earns more than Ian. Who earns the least money?

(a) Joan   (b) Rob   (c) Ian   (d) Michael   (e) Andrew

3   John, Fred, Steve and Jo all have similar jobs, although Fred and John are the only ones who have full-time work. John and Steve travel to work by train, but the others are lucky enough to be able to walk to work. Only John and Jo have cars. Who owns a car, but travels to work by train?

(a) John   (b) Fred   (c) Steve   (d) Jo

4   In the local tennis league a table shows how many games each member has won. Martin has won fewest games, followed in ascending order by Lisa, Karen and James, though Karen and James have won an equal number of games. Anne is one game ahead of Karen and James and Robert is two games ahead of Anne. Karen wins the next match. Who is now on the same level as Anne?

(a) Martin   (b) Lisa   (c) Karen   (d) James   (e) Robert

5   Caterers have been given a list of the special dietary requirements of some of the people attending a business lunch. Mr Reynolds and Ms Kelly eat fish and dairy products. Ms Wells and Mr Elcott eat vegetables and eggs. Mr Reynolds and Mr Elcott are the only ones who eat salad and fish. Which is the only food that Mr Elcott does not eat?

(a) fish   (b) dairy produce   (c) vegetables   (d) eggs   (e) salad

6   Mike, Barbara, Rachael, Jim and Colin all have PCs on their desks. Mike and
    Colin have printers on their desks. The other three have calculators. Mike and
    Jim have their desks in private offices, the other three work in an open-plan
    office. Who has a printer in a private office?

    (a) Mike   (b) Barbara   (c) Rachael   (d) Jim   (e) Colin

Answers

1   a

2   d

3   a

4   c

5   b

6   a

Numerical tests

This is just a quick mental warm-up for the David Singmaster tests that follow.

Numerical test 1

Find the next number in the series from one of the multiple choice answers of (a), (b), (c) or (d).

						(a)	(b)	(c)	(d)
1	4	8	12	16		(a) 20	(b) 22	(c) 24	(d) 12
2	.25	1	4	16		(a) 8	(b) 50	(c) 16	(d) 64
3	1	2	3	5		(a) 13	(b) 8	(c) 10	(d) 7
4	25	5	16	4	9	(a) 18	(b) 3	(c) 1,8	(d) 7
5	7	5	12	6	4	(a) 8	(b) 10	(c) 24	(d) 2
6	1	7	13	19	25	(a) 31	(b) 32	(c) 23	(d) 29
7	50	41	35	28	22	(a) 20	(b) 18	(c) 17	(d) 16
8	90	10	80	20	70	(a) 60	(b) 50	(c) 70	(d) 30
9	91	10	81	9	71	(a) 11	(b) 7	(c) 8	(d) 9
10	23	19	17	13		(a) 9	(b) 5	(c) 7	(d) 11

Answers

1	a	**6**	a
2	d	**7**	c
3	b	**8**	d
4	b	**9**	c
5	b	**10**	d

David Singmaster's problems

David Singmaster is a well-known mathematician and setter of perplexing problems. While you may not encounter questions exactly like these in aptitude tests, they provide an excellent intellectual work-out, since they demand logical thinking, lateral thinking and application of the knowledge you already possess. There are 15 problems below and the solutions follow on page 182.

Problems

Problem 1 Strange relationships in Much Puzzling

The village of Much Puzzling has a baker, a brewer and a butcher, like most villages. The other day I was talking to the baker's wife and she remarked that these three jobs were held by a Mr Baker, a Mr Brewer and a Mr Butcher, but no man held the job corresponding to his surname.

'But everyone knows that, even a newcomer like myself!' I responded.

But she continued, 'But I'll bet you don't know what Mrs Brewer told me just the other day. You see, each of the men married the sister of one of the other men. And no man married a girl of the same name as his occupation!'

'No, I hadn't known that. That's quite remarkable.'

What was the butcher's wife's maiden name?

Problem 2 Home is the Hunter

Hiawatha, the mighty hunter, has wandered far in search of game. One morning he has breakfast at his camp. He gets up and heads north. After going 10 miles in a straight line, he stops for lunch. He eats hurriedly, then gets up and again heads north. After going 10 miles in a straight line, he finds himself back at his morning's camp — honest Injun! Where on Earth is he?

Problem 3 The squashed fly

Two locomotives are heading towards one another from 100 miles apart on a straight track. The first is going at 60 mph and the second is going at 40 mph. A fly starts at the front of the first locomotive and flies to the second and then back to the first, then back to the second, etc. Eventually there is a terrible crash and our fly is squashed. If the fly can fly at 50 mph, how far does he fly before the smash?

Problem 4 Share and share alike

Jessica and her friend Pud like to eat a big lunch. One day Jessica brought four sandwiches and Pud brought five. Samantha got mugged on her way to school, but the mugger ran off with her lunch, although he left her purse. So Jessica and Pud shared their sandwiches with Samantha.

After eating, Samantha said, 'Thanks a million. I've got to see Mr Grind, but here's some money to pay for the sandwiches'. She left £3 and ran off.

Jessica said, 'Let me see, I brought four and you brought five, so I get 4/9 of £3, which is 4/3 of a pound, which is £1.33, near enough'.

Pud said, 'Ummm, I'm not sure that's fair'. Why?

Problem 5 Time flies

If I fly from London to New York at about 700 mph, then I keep up with the Earth's rotation and arrive at the same time that I left. If I go faster, say in Concorde, then I arrive in New York at an earlier hour than I departed from London.

Suppose we continue this all the way around the Earth. Then it seems that we arrive back in London before we start! What is wrong with this?

Problem 6 A striking problem

My village church clock strikes the hours and makes one stroke on the half-hours. The other night I had trouble sleeping. I woke up and lay there listening to the clock. What is the longest time I could have been awake before I knew what time it was? And what time(s) could it have been then?

Problem 7 Solid dominoes

Consider a 3 × 3 chessboard and a supply of dominoes that covers two adjacent cells of the board. Clearly one cannot cover the nine cells of the board with dominoes, but it is easy to cover the board if we omit the middle cell. Now consider a 3 × 3 × 3 array of cells and a supply of 'solid dominoes' or 'bicubes', i.e. blocks that cover two adjacent cubical cells of the array. Again we cannot expect to cover the 27 cells with solid dominoes, but can we do it if we omit the middle cell of the array?

Problem 8 Square cutting

Take any square sheet of paper, perhaps a paper napkin. Using one straight cut with scissors, divide it into four equal squares. Once you've done that, work out how to divide a similar square of paper into four equal triangles.

Problem 9 She's a square

Jessica's friend Katie says she will be x years old in the year x^2. How old was she in 2002?

Problem 10 A shorter century

Every reader of these problems already knows that the twenty-first century didn't start until 1 January 2001 because there wasn't a year 0. But do you know that the twenty-first century will be shorter than the twentieth century. Why?

Problem 11 A grave misunderstanding?

Salisbury Cathedral is one of the great glories of English architecture. While wandering through it, I came across a tomb slab in the North Choir Aisle with the following remarkable inscription:

Here lies the body of Tho the sonn of Tho.

Lambert gent who was borne May ye.13 AD. 1683 & dyed Feb 19 the same year.

How can this be?

Problem 12 Screwed up

A cylindrical helix is just a spiral on a cylinder, like an ordinary spring or the thread on a bolt. There are two kinds – a right-handed helix and a left-handed helix. If I turn a left-handed helix over (i.e. end for end), does it become a right-handed helix? Give as simple an explanation as you can.

Problem 13 Want a date?

Quickly now, what year was it 3000 years before 2002?

Problem 14 Half a cube

Some years ago, during the Rubik's Cube craze, the German firm of Togu made $2 \times 2 \times 2$ cubes with various colour patterns. The simplest one had four red cubelets and four blue cubelets. The advertising material said that there were 70 different patterns on this cube. This was based on the fact that we can choose four of the eight cells in a $2 \times 2 \times 2$ array in $8 \times 4 \times 4 = 70$ ways. However, these choices are not really all different. One such choice is to make the bottom half red and the top half blue and this is really the same thing as choosing any one of the six halves to be red. That is, there are six different choices that give the same pattern. So how many really different patterns are there?

Problem 15 Sum trouble

Jessica and her friend Hannah were looking at a puzzle book that asked how to put plus and minus signs into the sequence 123456789 in order to make it add up to 100. After a bit, they looked at the answer and found $1 + 2 + 3 - 4 + 5 + 6 + 78 + 9 = 100$.

Hannah said, 'I bet there are more ways to do this'.

Jessica replied, 'Sure, but I don't like that minus sign, it's too complicated. I'd rather have only plus signs. I wonder if that's possible'.

'If it were possible, they'd have asked for it', replied Hannah.

'Possibly. Or perhaps it's too easy', mused Jessica.

Who is right?

Solutions

Solution 1 Strange relationships in Much Puzzling

There are several ways to approach this. The simplest is to observe that the baker's wife cannot be Mrs Brewer (unless she talks to herself). She also cannot be Mrs Baker, since the baker is not Mr Baker. Hence she must be Mrs Butcher.

Now the brewer cannot be Mr Brewer and we have just seen that he cannot be Mr Butcher, so he must be Mr Baker and the butcher must be Mr Brewer.

Mr Brewer, the butcher, didn't marry his sister, Miss Brewer, nor did he marry Miss Butcher, so he must have married Miss Baker.

More generally, you can form a tabular arrangement of the surnames, jobs and wife's maiden names. There are just two arrangements compatible with the baker's wife's information. The fact that the baker's wife is not Mrs Brewer determines one of these arrangements. Indeed, any such piece of information determines the entire arrangement.

If the baker's wife does talk to herself, then she is Mrs Brewer and the other arrangement holds, in which Mr Baker, the butcher, mated Miss Brewer.

This problem uses simple logic, but most people find it useful to make a table of the situation.

Solution 2 Home is the hunter

This seems quite impossible, but is actually quite easy. Hiawatha is anywhere less than 10 miles from the North Pole, but not at the Pole. So when he heads north and goes 10 miles, he crosses over the Pole and continues a bit beyond. After lunch, he returns the way he came.

This problem requires you to extend your horizons. As stated, the problem seems impossible since you tend to think of any section of the Earth as being more or less flat and aligned with the four directions – north, east, south and west. You have to ask yourself where on earth does our normal conception break down. Once you make this 'aha' shift, the answer is easily found. Indeed the phrase 'where on Earth' has been included to help you to find the answer. Note that the problem also makes careful use of language. Hiawatha 'heads north and goes 10 miles' is carefully different than 'Hiawatha goes 10 miles north', but people often think incorrectly even when the correct phrase is repeated to them.

Solution 3 The squashed fly

If you answer 50 mph you are right in a way. The trains are approaching from 100 miles apart at a total speed of 100 mph, so they'll collide in just one hour, during which time our fly has flown 50 miles (no flies on him!).

But sadly, you're all wrong! Since the first train is going at 60 mph and the poor fly can only do 50 mph, he remains stuck fast on the front of the first locomotive, totally unable to do anything but stare at the oncoming disaster. Some people claim that the fly would be able to head away from the first locomotive at a total speed of 110 mph, but air resistance would keep him from getting more than a negligible distance.

The key idea is already expressed in the solution. This is a trick variation on a classic problem, dating back to about 1900. Many people know the problem when the fly can fly at 100 mph and hence leap into using the standard solution of that version, not noting the change of value of the fly's speed. Moral: don't solve your problem until you've read it very carefully!

Solution 4 Share and share alike

Since they shared the sandwiches, they each ate three sandwiches and so each sandwich is worth £1. So Jessica gave one sandwich to Samantha while Pud gave two, so Jessica should get £1 and Pud should get £2.

This is a classic, dating back to at least 1202, but people have trouble figuring out how to proceed. The key ideas are to examine the distribution of the sandwiches and to determine the value of a sandwich.

Solution 5 Time flies

One actually can arrive back in New York at an earlier hour than one leaves, but it is on the next day. We cross the International Date Line.

Again, this initially seems to be an impossibility, but we soon realize there must be somewhere where the argument breaks down. For this question you do need a small amount of special knowledge, namely that there is an International Date Line. Incidentally, though the idea was developed around 1300, the Date Line was not adopted until 1884.

Solution 6 A striking problem

I could have been awake for an hour and a half and it could then be either 1.30 or 2.00. This can happen in two ways:

■ I could have woken up as I heard one stroke. Not knowing whether it was part of an hour or not, it could be any time. After half an hour, I hear one stroke. Then I know it is either a half-hour or 1.00. After a second half-hour, I hear a single stroke again. Then I know it must be either 1.00 or 1.30, but I won't know which until I hear the clock after another half-hour – if I then hear a fourth consecutive single stroke, it is 1.30, while if I then hear two strokes, it is 2.00.

■ Alternatively, I might have woken up just after the clock struck, without hearing it. After half an hour, I hear one stroke and the situation is the same as the above. However, in this case, I do not get to hear four consecutive single strokes and I have waited perhaps a second less than in the previous case.

This is probably best done by trial and error, using the observation that the answer must involve one o'clock in some way.

Solution 7 Solid dominoes

No, it cannot be done. View the $3 \times 3 \times 3$ array as a three-dimensional chess-board, with the cells alternately coloured black and white. Suppose the corners are coloured black. Then the layers look like the following.

BWB	WBW	BWB
WBW	BWB	WBW
BWB	WBW	BWB

There are $5 + 4 + 5 = 14$ black cells and $4 + 5 + 4 = 13$ white cells. Now when we remove the middle cell, we are removing a white cell and leaving a pattern of 14 black and 12 white cells. Since a domino covers one black and one white cell, no matter where it is placed, no collection of dominoes can cover the board with the middle deleted.

Solution 8 Square cutting

Fold the square along a diagonal. Fold the resulting triangle in half, along the bisector of its right angle, which is along the other diagonal of the original square. This yields another right-angled triangle having both the vertical and horizontal midlines of the square lying along the bisector of the right angle of the triangle. Hence a single cut along this bisector will produce four squares.

To divide into four triangles, fold the square in half to make the diagonals lie together, rather than the midlines. This is done by simply folding along one midline, then the other, to yield a square, and then cut along the diagonal that passes through the corner which was the original centre of the square.

Solution 9 She's a square

The only square year in the near future is 2025 (45^2). Hence Katie was born in 1980 and she will be 22 years old in 2002.

Solution 10 A shorter century

The year 2000 was a leap year, but the year 2100 is not, so the twentieth century is a day longer. (The twenty-first century will be lengthened by a few 'leap seconds' to compensate for the fact that the Earth is running a bit slow, so it will be a bit less than a day shorter.) This uses a little specialized knowledge, but the fact should be fairly well known to everyone who has lived through the recent millennium muddles. Incidentally, Ruth Rendell's Inspector Wexford detected a literary forgery that claimed to be a diary, because it had the date 29 February 1900 in it.

Solution 11 A grave misunderstanding?

The explanation lies not in ourselves but in our stars – or rather in our calendars. From the early Middle Ages until the adoption of the Gregorian calendar in 1582, the new year began on 25th of March. Hence dates up to 25 March were considered as part of the previous year. Because of religious differences, England did not adopt the Gregorian calendar until 1751, after the death of young Thomas Lambert.

Because of the difference between English and continental dates during 1582–1751, you must be cautious with English historical dates that occur on I January to 24 March in these years. Indeed, you sometimes see English dates of this period written as 1 Feb 1691/2, meaning that some people thought it was 1691 while others thought it was 1692. To confuse matters even more, Scotland changed to using 1 January as the beginning of the year in 1600, though it didn't adopt the Gregorian calendar.

Solution 12 Screwed up

The handedness remains the same when it is turned over. You may be able to see this mentally, but otherwise consider putting a nut on a bolt. If the handedness of a helix changed in turning it over, then half the time we tried to put a nut on, it wouldn't fit and we would have to turn it over. But we know this isn't true – it doesn't matter which end of the nut is up.

The problem here is that very few people can visualize the process carefully, so you have to search for some other way to demonstrate the result. Here we have to resort to real-world instances of a mathematical concept, so the idea of a bolt was given in the problem.

Solution 13 Want a date?

In 2002 one year ago was 2001, two years ago was 2000, and 2002 years ago was 0, so 3000 years ago was 998, i.e. 998 BC. Unfortunately this is wrong — it was 999 BC because there wasn't a year 0! When Dionysius Exiguus set out the calendar in the sixth century, zero hadn't become known in Europe and so he omitted a year 0. Thus the year before AD 1 is 1 BC.

This is a trick problem dependent on special knowledge – but knowledge that most people have.

Solution 14 Half a cube

Let the four cells or cubelets on the bottom level be numbered 1, 2, 3 and 4 in cyclic order and let the cells above them be 5, 6, 7 and 8 in the same order. We can always turn the cube so that cell 1 is one of the chosen cells, i.e. is red.

Let us consider the largest clump (or component) of adjacent chosen or red cells. If there are at least three cells in this clump, then we can bring three of them into positions 1, 2 and 3. Then we see that all five choices of a fourth cell give dif-ferent patterns.

Now suppose our largest clump has two adjacent cells. We can bring these into positions 1 and 2. Now we can't choose 3, 4, 5 or 6 as that gives a larger clump, so the only case here is 1, 2, 7 and 8 – two parallel double cubes.

Finally, suppose no two cells are adjacent. There is essentially just one such pattern: 1, 3, 6, 8. This gives a total of seven patterns – much smaller than the 70 claimed!

The patterns 1, 2, 3, 5 and 1, 2, 3, 7 are mirror images, which might be con-sidered the same in some problems, but here we are dealing with a real physical cube so we cannot reflect it. (Notice that in each pattern the red cells are congru-ent to the blue cells. It is also true that every division of the 2×2 square into two red and two blue cells has the red cells congruent to the blue cells. However this does not continue into higher dimensions.)

This is a straightforward systematic case of trial and error. The difficult part is seeing how to account for the possible movements of the cube and how to break down the examination into manageable parts.

Solution 15 Sum trouble

Hannah is right – there is no way to insert just plus signs into the sequence to make it add up to 100. You have to use the ancient technique of 'casting out nines', or the more modern equivalent of congruence (mod 9). For those who don't know or don't remember this, the idea is that any number is congruent to the sum of its digits and that the arithmetic operations +, – and $\times$ are preserved by this con-gruence. For example, 21 is congruent to (adds up to) 3 and 32 is congruent to (adds up to) 5. So $21 + 32 = 53$ is congruent to $3 + 5 = 8$.

If the sum of the digits is greater than 9, we can repeat the process. For example, 58 is congruent to $(5 + 8 =) 13$, which is congruent to $(1 + 3 =) 4$. We also have that 9 is congruent to 0. Now we also have $21 - 32 = -11$ is congruent to $(3 - 5 =) -2$, which is congruent to 7. And $21 \times 32 = 672$ is congruent to $3 \times 5 = 15$, which is congruent to $(1 + 5 =) 6$.

Another way to form the sum of the digits is simply to 'cast out a nine' each time the sum exceeds 9. For example, if we consider 672 and say 6 + 7 is 13, casting out 9 leaves 4, 4 + 2 is 6.

How does this apply to Jessica's problem? Quite easily. No matter how we insert plus signs, the terms will contain all the digits 1, 2 ... 9 and the sum of the terms will hence be congruent to the sum of these digits (mod 9). But $1 + 2 + \ldots \pm 9 = 45$, which is congruent to 9 or 0, while 100 is congruent to 1. So no sum with digits 1, 2 ... 9 can add up to 100, not even if we reorder them. Observe that the solution given had a −4 instead of a +4, which had the effect of subtracting 8 and so the sum of the numbers and the sum of the digits comes out $9 - 8 = 1$ (mod 9) as required.

Saville and Holdsworth tests

Ability tests are frequently used by employers as part of the selection process. You could be asked to complete one of a number of different types of ability test. The following verbal reasoning, numerical reasoning and diagrammatic reasoning tests have been developed by Saville and Holdsworth, a talent management company that provides assessment and development solutions to help companies make the most of their human resources. Items from several types of test are included to give you some practice in answering a variety of questions. The answers are provided on page 203.

Verbal reasoning tests

This section consists of a series of passages, each of which is followed by several statements. Your task is to evaluate each statement in the light of the passage that precedes it, and to decide whether each statement is true, false, or you cannot say without further information. Time yourself and see how many exercises you can do in eight minutes.

Passage 1

Many dual-career parents are concerned about arrangements for their children during the summer months when the children are at home. There are several ways that employers can cope with this problem: allowing the dual wife or husband to have a lighter load during these months, allowing the dual wife or husband to build up a backlog of working time during other months to relieve them during the summer months, providing facilities on site during the summer months for young children (perhaps using students training in the field of primary education), or some combination of all of these. However, building up a backlog of working time has generally proved difficult to achieve.

Statements

Mark each statement as true/false/cannot say without further information:

1 Increasingly, both parents of children are pursuing their own careers.

2 Students training in primary education can assist with the provision of arrangements for children during the summer holidays.

3 The best solution to the problem is to lighten the workload of one or both of the parents during the summer months.

4 Building up a backlog of working time is an easy-to-implement solution for coping with the problem of working parents' summer arrangements.

Passage 2

Computing technology undoubtedly makes it possible for more people to spend more time working at home. It is easier nowadays to obtain information at home and to communicate with the workplace. Telecommuting, where people work predominantly at or from home and stay in touch using the phone, personal computer, fax, e-mail, internet or videoconferencing, is becoming increasingly common in some professions.

Statements

Mark each statement as true/false/cannot say without further information:

5 Telecommuting increases the efficiency of work.

6 The advance of technology has increased the possibility for sales representatives to spend time working away from the office.

7 Internet access is necessary for telecommuters to stay in touch.

8 People who do work from home can keep in touch with the workplace using phone, fax, e-mail and videoconferencing.

Passage 3

Mensa was founded in 1946, after a chance meeting on a train between an Oxford postgraduate called Lancelot Ware and Roland Berrill, a 50-year-old Australian of private means. The two men discovered a mutual interest in IQ testing. When Ware tested Berrill and announced that he was in the top 1 per cent of the population, the latter is said to have burst into tears. He was rejected by Oxford and this was the very first time he had ever been told that he was good at anything. From that day forward, the reassurance of the insecure has always been an inseparable part of Mensa's operations. However, that wasn't the aim of Mensa. It was intended to be a contact organization and research body – and there was always the notion that a useful chain reaction might occur with a critical mass of brainpower.

Statements

Mark each as true/false/cannot say without further information:

9 Lancelot Ware and Roland Berrill arranged to meet on the train in 1946.

10 Ware's IQ was in the top 1 per cent.

11 One of Mensa's aims was to be a research body.

12 There was no IQ testing in Australia in 1946.

Passage 4

New technology can affect greatly the amount and nature of social interaction experienced by staff in an organization. Some of the ways this happens are easy to imagine. Well-established work groups may be broken up, redundancies may occur, communication may become less face-to-face and more computer-mediated, and the sheer amount of information conveyed by the new technology may replace the need for interpersonal communication of any kind.

Statements

Mark each as true/false/cannot say without further information:

13 The introduction of new technology is likely to reduce social interaction.

14 Social interaction among staff is important in the running of any organization.

15 Experienced staff need less social interaction.

16 Communication may become more impersonal with the introduction of new technology.

Numerical reasoning tests

You may be asked to answer different types of numerical reasoning questions. These could consist of a table or chart displaying various facts and figures to which you need to refer. Alternatively, you may be presented with a series of number sequences, each of which has one number missing, which you have to replace from the options provided.

Numerical test type 1

This section consists of a number of statistical tables displaying various facts and figures, to which you will need to refer in order to answer the questions. For each question you are given five options to choose from. One and only one of the options is correct in each case. Your task is to decide which of these is the correct one.

You may wish to use rough paper and a calculator for this section. See how many questions you can answer in 15 minutes.

Table 1   Cement production, delivery and imports (thousands of tonnes)

Date	Quarter	Production	Deliveries	Imports
2002	Q1	2 786	2 781	307
	Q2	3 122	3 014	290
2001	Q1	3 016	2 976	357
	Q2	3 369	3 120	382
	Q3	3 242	3 097	349
	Q4	2 845	2 661	312
	Total	12 474	11 754	1 400
2000	Q1	2 918	2 814	228
	Q2	3 331	3 062	235
	Q3	3 364	3 108	278
	Q4	3 084	2 752	408
	Total	12 697	11 736	1 149

1   How many more tonnes of cement were produced than delivered in the first quarter of 2001 (in thousands of tonnes)?

(a) 5   (b) 40   (c) 104   (d) 249   (e) Cannot say

2   What percentage of the total imported cement in 2000 was imported in the third quarter?

(a) 19.8%   (b) 20.4%   (c) 24.2%   (d) 35.5%   (e) Cannot say

3   How does cement production in 2002 compare with that in 2001?

(a) Decrease by 47%   (b) Decrease by 7.5%   (c) Increase by 7.5%
(d) Increase by 47%   (e) Cannot say

Table 2 Participation in education and training of 16-year-olds

	1999	2000	2001
Full-time education (%)	69.4	69.8	71.2
Maintained schools (%)	*28.0*	*28.2*	*28.5*
Independent schools (%)	*6.4*	*6.3*	*6.2*
Further education (%)	*35.0*	*35.3*	*36.4*
Other education and training (%)	17.2	16.8	15.5
Not in any education or training (%)	14.2	14.2	14.0
Number of 16-year-olds (thousands)	610.0	600.4	609.1

4 In 2000, approximately how many 16-year-olds were not in any education or training?

(a) 45 250   (b) 50 550   (c) 62 000   (d) 85 250

(e) None of these

5 How many more 16-year-olds were there in full-time education in 2001, compared to 2000?

(a) 160   (b) 1 460   (c) 1 600   (d) 14 600   (e) 16 000

6 In 1999, approximately what proportion of 16-year-olds in full-time education were in independent schools?

(a) 6%   (b) 9%   (c) 11%   (d) 14%   (e) 19%

7 Which type(s) of full-time education showed a year-on-year decrease in the proportion of 16-year-old students between 1999 and 2001?

(a) Maintained schools   (b) Independent schools   (c) Further education

(d) All of them   (e) None of them

Table 3 Driving test applications and results (thousands of applicants)

	2000	2001
Applications received	1607.9	1631.4
Tests conducted	1482.9	1489.0
Tests passed	697.4	684.2

8 Approximately, what percentage of applications received in 2000 resulted in tests being conducted?

(a) 84%   (b) 87%   (c) 92%   (d) 95%   (e) 97%

9 How many more tests were failed in 2001 than 2000?

(a) 1 930   (b) 2 010   (c) 15 700   (d) 19 300   (e) 20 100

10 By approximately what percentage did the number of applications received in 2001 increase from the previous year?

(a) 1.5%   (b) 3.2%   (c) 4.7%   (d) 10.1%   (e) 11.5%

11 If the pass rate falls by 1% per year between 2001 and 2005, how many passes will there be in 2005?

(a) 62 380   (b) 65 720   (c) 623 800   (d) 657 200
(e) Cannot say

Table 4 Emissions of carbon dioxide by source (figures in millions of tonnes)

	1995–97	1998–2000
Industrial combustion	111	108
Power stations	162	132
Transport	105	108
Domestic	72	69
Other sources	33	36

12 What was the total number of tonnes of carbon dioxide emitted by power stations between 1995 and 2000?

(a) 2 650 000　　(b) 2 940 000　　(c) 3 890 000　　(d) 265 000 000

(e) 294 000 000

13 What was the approximate change in total carbon dioxide emissions between 1995–97 and 1998–2000?

(a) Decrease by 6%　　(b) Decrease by 5%　　(c) Decrease by 2%

(d) Increase by 4%　　(e) Increase by 5%

14 If the proportion of carbon dioxide emissions from domestic sources decreased to 10% in 2001–3, what would be the total number of tonnes emitted from domestic sources in 2001–3?

(a) 39 000 000　　(b) 46 000 000　　(c) 52 000 000　　(d) 64 000 000

(e) Cannot-say

15 In 1998–2000, approximately what proportion of carbon dioxide emissions were from industrial combustion and power stations combined?

(a) 48%　　(b) 53%　　(c) 57%　　(d) 67%　　(e) 80%

16 If emissions from power stations decrease by 10% in each of the next four three-year periods, what will they be in 2010–12?

(a) 71 800 000　　(b) 79 200 000　　(c) 86 600 000

(d) 94 000 000　　(e) Cannot say

Numerical test type 2

This section consists of a series of number sequences, each of which has one number missing.

For each question you are given five options to choose from to replace the missing number. One and only one of the options is correct in each case. Your task is to decide which of these is the correct one.

1	3	?	17	24		(a) 4	(b) 5	(c) 7	(d) 9	(e) 10
2	5	6	9	14	?	(a) 17	(b) 18	(c) 21	(d) 24	(e) 25
3	40.6	36.4	?	28		(a) 30	(b) 30.2	(c) 31.6	(d) 32	(e) 32.2

Diagrammatic reasoning tests

You could be presented with several different types of diagrammatic reasoning questions. The items could consist of a series of diagrams for which you have to choose the next diagram in the series. Alternatively, you could be presented with figures, digits or letters that are then transformed by various commands. You either have to decide what transformations the commands are performing or what the outcome of transformations are.

Diagrammatic test type 1

Each problem in this section consists of a series of diagrams on the left of the page, which follow a logical sequence. You are to choose the next diagram in the series from the five options on the right. See how many you can complete in four minutes.

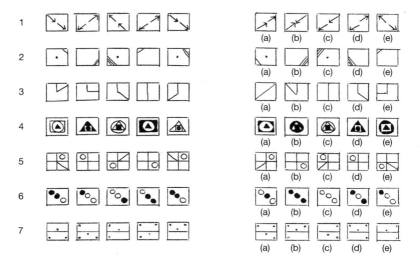

Diagrammatic test type 2

In this section, figures within boxes are presented in columns and are changed in some way by various commands contained in circles.

Each problem consists of several figures in a column. Work down the column, starting at the top and dealing with each command and adjacent figure in turn. You must choose from the five possible answers provided on the right-hand side of the page – the column that results from carrying out the given commands.

Key to commands:

⊗ invert figure

⊕ reverse figure

⟳ rotate figure clockwise by 90°

⟲ rotate figure anticlockwise by 90°

◎ omit figure

⬍ exchange contents of this box with contents of previous box

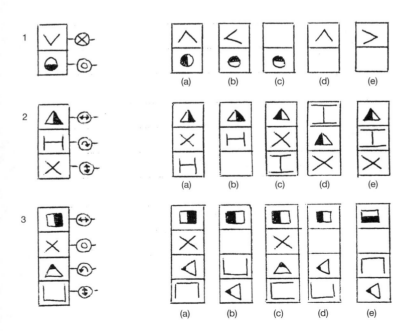

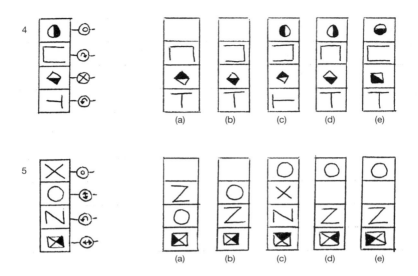

4

5

(a) (b) (c) (d) (e)

Diagrammatic test type 3

In this section there are a number of diagrams. Within each diagram, sequences of digits are altered in some ways by various commands. The commands are represented by symbols. For example:

$$890 \longrightarrow \odot \longrightarrow 8890$$

In this example the command $\odot$ doubles the first digit of the sequence.

Your task is to work through a diagram, following paths that are indicated by sets of arrows, in order to determine the effect of the commands and then to answer the questions that follow each diagram.

When tracing a path between two sequences, you must follow a path that includes only one colour of arrow.

Note that each symbol has a different meaning. If the same symbol occurs more than once in a diagram, it has the same meaning each time. However, the meanings of the symbols may differ from one diagram to the next.

See how many you can do in 12 minutes.

Diagram 1

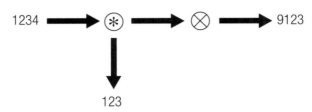

1 2468 ⟹ (✳) ⟹ ?

   (a) 248   (b) 9246   (c) 9468   (d) 92468   (e) 2469

2 321 ⟹ ⊗ ⟹ ?

   (a) 123   (b) 9123   (c) 1239   (d) 9321   (e) 3219

3 3456 ⟹ ⊗ ⟹ (✳) ⟹ ?

   (a) 345   (b) 9456   (c) 3459   (d) 4569   (e) 9345

Diagram 2

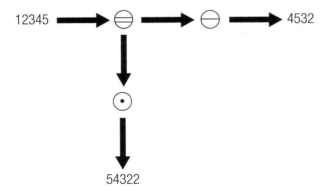

4 1357 ⟹ ⊖ ⟹ ?

   (a) 11357   (b) 13577   (c) 7531   (d) 3157   (e) 1375

5 3521 ⟹ ⊖ ⟹ ?

   (a) 35211   (b) 33521   (c) 1253   (d) 5321   (e) 5312

6 2368 ⟹ ⊙ ⟹ ⊖ ⟹ ?

(a) 6832   (b) 8632   (c) 32688   (d) 86322   (e) 88632

7 7891 ⟹ ⊙ ⟹ ? ⟹ 87911

(a) ⊙   (b) ⊖   (c) ⊖   (d) ⊖   (e) ⊖ ⟹ ⊖

Diagram 3

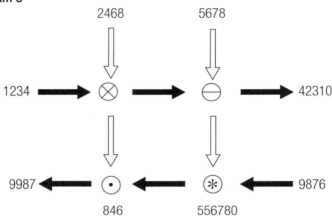

8 3079 ⟹ ⊙ ⟹ ?

(a) 30790   (b) 33079   (c) 9073   (d) 9703   (e) 307

9 6513 ⟹ ✳ ⟹ ⊖ ⟹

(a) 65   (b) 5513   (c) 5130   (d) 6510   (e) 665130

10 1927 ⟹ ? ⟹ 71921

(a) ⊗   (b) ✳⟹⊗   (c) ⊗⟹⊗   (d) ⊙⟹✳⟹⊙

(e) ⊗⟹✳⟹⊗

11 7319 ⟹ ? ⟹ 137

(a) ⊙   (b) ⊗⟹⊙   (c) ⊙⟹⊗   (d) ⊙⟹⊗

(e) ⊙⟹⊗⟹⊗

Answers

Verbal

1	Cannot say	9	False
2	True	10	Cannot say
3	Cannot say	11	True
4	False	12	Cannot say
5	Cannot say	13	True
6	Cannot say	14	Cannot say
7	False	15	Cannot say
8	True	16	True

Numerical

Numerical type 1:

1	b	9	d
2	c	10	a
3	e	11	e
4	d	12	e
5	d	13	a
6	b	14	e
7	b	15	b
8	c	16	c

Numerical type 2:

1 e

2 c

3 e

Diagrammatic

Diagrammatic type 1:

1	d	**5**	d
2	b	**6**	e
3	e	**7**	a
4	b		

Diagrammatic type 2:

1	d	**4**	a
2	c	**5**	e
3	b		

Diagrammatic type 3:

1	a	**7**	c
2	d	**8**	e
3	e	**9**	e
4	d	**10**	b
5	c	**11**	c
6	e		

The Work Style Questionnaire.

The following questionnaire will give you an idea of your work style and may help you build on knowledge you already have about those working situations in which you are most effective and those which you find more difficult. After completing the questionnaire, you may find it helpful to look again at Chapter 11 on reflecting on your test performance.

Look at each of the statements below and rate them on a scale of 1 to 5

1 = Strongly disagree

5 = Strongly agree

	Statement	Rating	
1	I am happiest when I can implement my own ideas		IND
2	I don't like working on my own		SOC
3	I am often the one to come up with new ideas		CRE
4	I like paying attention to detail		REL
5	I don't like a predictable work routine		CRE
6	I work most effectively if there are ample opportunities to share ideas with colleagues		CO
7	I like to have the freedom to try out new ideas, even if there is a risk that they may be unsuccessful		IND
8	I believe that colleagues would describe me as a reliable person to work with		REL
9	I never have trouble coming up with suggestions		CRE
10	I like taking decisions at work		INF
11	I work most effectively if I am left to get on with my tasks without interference		IND
12	I seek out opportunities to take responsibility		AMB

	Statement	Rating	
13	Having good working relationships with my colleagues is very important to me		SOC
14	I am often the one to organize an event such as a leaving do or an office outing		SOC
15	Having work which offers plenty of opportunities for advancement is important to me		AMB
16	I am always prepared to try a new approach		CRE
17	I encourage other people to contribute suggestions and ideas		CO
18	I dislike having to complete tasks in a hurry		REL
19	Being respected by colleagues is very important to me		PER
20	I expect my own efforts to be rewarded financially or with promotion		AMB
21	I find it difficult to deal with confrontations at work		UC
22	I work hard and I expect to gain promotion rapidly		AMB
23	It really matters to me that family, friends and colleagues value the job I do and the progress I make		AMB
24	I only thrive if my work is frequently praised		UC
25	I get a lot of satisfaction from persuading someone to see a problem from my point of view – I like winning an argument		INF
26	I listen carefully to what others are saying		CO
27	I don't usually offer an opinion at work unless it is deliberately sought		UC
28	I can usually motivate other people by being enthusiastic myself		INF
29	I pay great attention to details like punctuality and time keeping		REL

	Statement	Rating
30	I find it difficult to accept criticism	UC
31	I thrive on change and on being asked to do something new or get a project started	CRE
32	I shall only be happy when I get to the top in my chosen profession	AMB
33	I like following things up and researching information	EVA
34	Even when working in a team, I still like to have the ultimate responsibility for decisions	IND
35	I think I can easily spot and take advantage of new opportunities	CRE
36	I don't mind being unpopular if it leads to good results	CT
37	I can often persuade people to do something in a different way from the tried and tested	INF
38	I think colleagues my sometimes view me as rather forceful	CT
39	I do not make careless mistakes with my work	REL
40	I believe people are motivated by feeling encouraged	CO
41	I am probably a bit of a perfectionist	CT
42	I can influence the decision making process effectively, even when I don't take the decision myself	INF
43	I enjoy analysing problems and situations and looking at all the options	EVA
44	I like being given difficult tasks, I see them as a challenge	VAR
45	I do tend to get bored easily and then my attention to detail may slip	VAR
46	I often find that colleagues confide in me	SOC
47	I like working to targets, but I like to set them myself	IND

	Statement	Rating
48	I find I settle into a new job quickly and easily	VAR
49	I will sometimes give in even if I don't agree just to avoid falling out with people	UC
50	I never put off difficult tasks – I like to deal with them straight away	PER
51	I enjoy those working days where you just never know what is going to happen next	VAR
52	To me the best part of work is forming good relationships with customers and colleagues	CO
53	I take advantage of any training opportunities that are on offer	PER
54	I enjoy seeing other staff develop and improve	CO
55	If I am having a problem with a colleague I try to address it straight away, rather than letting a problem build up	SOC
56	I never find myself doing things at the last minute	CT
57	If I have got a problem with something I don't mind admitting it	PER
58	I am prepared to work hard to see something through	PER
59	I think regular appraisals at work are very important	CT
60	I keep pretty calm in a crisis	REL
61	I view work as the most important part of my life	AMB
62	I could never stay in a job where I felt bored	VAR
63	I need to be able to use my professional knowledge and skills	PER
64	I like integrating and managing the efforts of others	INF
65	I need to see the results of my work	EVA
66	I cope well with constantly changing demands	VAR

	Statement	Rating	
67	I plan a job carefully before I make a start		EVA
68	The idea of routine really depresses me		VAR
69	I really enjoy gathering information and data		EVA
70	If I say I will do something, then I do it		REL
71	I take opportunities to train and teach other members of staff		INF
72	I often socialize with colleagues outside working hours		SOC
73	I really hate it if I upset somebody at work		UN
74	I believe people work most effectively if they are told exactly what to do		CT
75	I try hard to encourage quiet colleagues to contribute to discussions and meetings		CO
76	I am usually the first to arrive and the last to leave		CT
77	I prefer the idea of becoming a specialist to that of becoming a general manager		PER
78	I really need to take responsibility for organizing my own workload		IND
79	I like to have all the stages of a project clearly mapped out		EVA
80	I would really rather run my own business than work for someone else		IND
81	I will often check out my ideas with a colleague before I raise them with a larger group		UC
82	I believe that time spent thinking before taking action is time very well spent		EVA
83	I really enjoy striking up new relationships with customers and clients		SOC
84	I sometimes come up with unusual suggestions and I don't mind being laughed at, if it helps people try a new approach		CRE

To obtain your score, add up the scores for each group of questions which has the same symbol and enter them below:-

Symbol	Score
AMB	
CRE	
CO	
CT	
EVA	
IND	
INF	
PER	
REL	
SOC	
UC	
VAR	

Add an extra 5 points to your top score – this helps distinguish what is most significant for you, especially if you have produced similar scores across several of the characteristics. Here are the profiles for each characteristic.

AMB – Ambitious

Success in professional, financial and status terms is a key factor for you and is likely to influence how you operate at work. Your drive and energy are very useful for seeing projects through and making sure targets are met. Your focus on your own success is likely to have a down side too – you may not pay as much attention to the views and ideas of colleagues as you could.

CO – Co-operative

Co-operative people are very focused on the team and on getting the best out of other people, as well as themselves. As a co-operative person, you will often be the one who helps teams to jell, as you are likely to be able to encourage even the quieter members of a team to bring their ideas and suggestions to situations. If there is a downside it may be that you become more interested in the team functioning as a successful unit, than on the end goal.

CRE – Creative and imaginative

Creative people bring ideas to the work place and their infectious enthusiasm can often rub off on the whole team. As a creative person, you are likely to have imaginative ideas about how problems should be solved or how a new direction can be pursued. If you have a fault, it is that it is sometimes difficult for you to accept realistic restraints, such as resource implications. You may be keen to come up with plenty of ideas, but a bit more reluctant when it comes to seeing them through by paying attention to detail and concentrating on the job in hand.

CT – Controlling

The controlling people are exactly that – they need to feel that everything is under control and in good order and this generally applies as much to their own work as it does to the work of those around them. You are likely to be very concerned with detail and procedures and although this sounds dull, it can actually be very useful, especially in ensuring that important procedures are followed or that a project does not get lost because no one is paying attention to the more routine aspects of the work. Of course the down side is that you can lose sight of the greater vision and you can be extremely irritating to colleagues and rather difficult to work for if you are in a management or supervisory position.

EVA – Evaluative

Evaluators are often the calm, rational members of a work team, unlikely to go off on some of the wilder tangents pursued by their creative colleagues. You are likely to be good at researching and gathering information, weighing it up and making constructive suggestions about what is likely to work and what might not. Of course, there is the possible disadvantage that you may be determined not to act until you have all the appropriate information to make the best possible decision and you will argue for the most common sense course of action – occasionally losing the opportunity for something more risky, but perhaps more successful.

IND – Independent

Independent people value autonomy at work above all things – freedom to implement their own ideas and in their own way. If this is you are likely to have a lot of energy and enthusiasm, so long as you are left to do things in your own way and like your creative colleagues you may bring new and imaginative ways of looking at a problem. You may find it hard to work co-operatively and your colleagues may be annoyed because you seem to get away with things that they can't. You tend to pass by some of the constructive suggestions made by other people.

INF – Influencing and persuading

These people are very good at persuading others to buy something or do something. They are not simply good at the "hard sell"; they enjoy bringing subtle influences to bear too and can often have a very strong impact in a team. If you are an influencer you may now always come up with the ideas, but once you are convinced that an idea really is a good one, you are likely to affect its chances of being implemented. Managers like to have you on-side and if you are a manager, you should not have too hard a time keeping your team interested and involved. For you, winning an argument can occasionally become more important than the actual merits of that argument.

PER – Persistent Professional

These people work hard and their real interest is in building up specialist knowledge and expertise and being able to apply this. If this is you, you are likely to work hard for success, but see this in terms of professional development and respect from colleagues, rather than in straightforward terms of financial reward or promotion. You may tend to distance yourself from some of the day-to-day activities in the department, but you will always be happy to give advice.

REL – Reliable

Reliable people keep businesses functioning and reliable does not equate with boring. If you are reliable you are likely to be trusted and valued by colleagues and managers. You get on with things and will see a project through to the end without showing the obsessive qualities of the controller. You can sometimes get passed by for promotion on the grounds that other people have decided you are quite content where you are.

SO – Sociable

Sociable people are not necessarily the same as co-operative people, though it is more than possible to be both of these. Sociable people will not stay in a job if they don't like the people and/or the environment, so they are usually a cheerful a positive influence around the office. If you are sociable one of your real strengths is making new relationships with other departments, customers or clients and you are always the first to welcome new members to the team. You can tend to get so interested in organizing office outings or chatting to people to find out what is going on, that work gets pushed to the back seat.

VAR – Variety and risk

People who score highly here need variety and some unpredictability in their work in order to thrive. If this is you, you are often very valuable at times of change, because where other colleagues may see this as a source for stress and anxiety, you will see it as an opportunity or a challenge and some of your attitude will rub off on others. You are willing to have a go and if things go wrong, you will not lose too much sleep over it. Of course, you do get bored quickly and you will often resist carrying out the more routine aspects of your work and find yourself working in a slightly chaotic way.

UC – Under confidant

Under confident people are by no means under competent, though they sometimes tend to feel that this is the case. If this is you, you probably have plenty of good ideas, but you are unwilling to express them. You will find that colleagues trust you and may well seek you out to test their own ideas on someone, so you tend to use these opportunities to get your ideas drawn into the team and the system. You do run the danger of being viewed as disinterested.

The balanced worker

Of course, everyone is a mixture of all the above to various extents and there are also many other dimensions that make up the working you: your experience so far, how important a role work plays in your life and, very importantly, who you are working with in any team or department at any one time – all these are powerful influences. If some of the above does ring true for you, use it as a learning experience If there are things you would like to change, consider ways in which you could achieve this. If you are quite happy with the way that you work then of course, continue as you are.

part three

sources of information

General information
Equal opportunities information
Test practice information

Sources of information

General information

British Psychological Society

The BPS Occupational Psychologists Division provides lots of useful information. It publishes annual directories, which include reviews of all the major personality tests and aptitude tests currently being used. These books are expensive, but may be available at some university libraries and good reference libraries. Test reviews are currently being put on to the society's new psychological testing website (www.psychtesting.org.uk). The test reviews are helpful for employers who are considering using aptitude and personality tests in their selection processes.

The BPS also produces a booklet called *Psychological Testing, a Test Taker's Guide*. This includes information on testing in all settings, with sections on occupational testing, information about preparing for tests, obtaining results, and codes of practice for both test users and test takers.

Contact: British Psychological Society
Address: St Andrews House
                 48 Princess Road East
                 Leicester LE1 7DR
Tel: 0116 254 9568
Website: www.bps.org.uk

British Institute of Graphologists

Provides information on all aspects of handwriting analysis. It offers advice to employers who are considering using graphology and also to anyone who wishes to obtain an analysis of their own handwriting to find out what sort of profile it produces.

Contact:	British Institute of Graphologists
Address:	24–26 High Street
	Hampton Hill
	Middlesex TW12 1PD
Tel:	01753 891 241
Website:	www.britishgraphology.org

Equal opportunities information
Commission for Racial Equality

Provides information and codes of practice for employers to help them avoid discrimination in their recruitment and selection processes. It can also provide advice to individuals who feel they may have been discriminated against.

Contact:	Commission for Racial Equality
Address:	10–12 Allington Street
	London SW1E 5EH
Tel:	020 7828 7022
Website:	www.cre.gov.uk

Equal Opportunities Commission

Provides guidance to employers on all aspects of gender equality in the work place. It produces codes of practice and can also give advice to individuals who feel they may have been discriminated against.

Contact:	Equal Opportunities Commission
Address:	Arndale House
	Arndale Centre
	Manchester M4 3EQ
Tel:	0845 602 9601
Website:	www.eoc.org.uk

The Disability Rights Commission

Provides information on employment and the Disability Discrimination Act.

Contact:	The Disability Rights Commission
Address:	Freepost MD02164
	Stratford upon Avon CV37 9HY
Tel:	08457 622644
Website:	www.drc.gb.org.uk

Royal National Institute for the Blind

Can help employers to choose fair and appropriate selection methods and also works with some test developers and publishers to look at alternative ways of presenting test material.

Contact:	RNIB
Address:	104 Judd Street
	London WC1H 9NC
Tel:	020 7388 1266
Website:	www.rnib.org.uk

The Dyslexia Institute

Advises on any issue connected with dyslexia.

Contact:	The Dyslexia Institute
Address:	2 Grosvenor Gardens
	London SW1W 0DH
Tel:	020 7730 0273
Website:	dyslexia-inst.org.uk

Test practice information

Some employers who use selection tests do send out a few sample questions to applicants who have been invited to a test session. Please note that this information will only be sent to applicants who have been invited to a test.

University careers services

Many university careers services run practice test sessions for current and recent graduates. Some may charge for this service, especially to past graduates, but this is not likely to be as expensive as having tests done privately. It is certainly worth following up if you are currently a student, or have graduated within the last two years.

The Prospects website

The website at www.prospects.ac.uk contains a very useful section of psychometric testing. You can only access this site through a password system since it is geared to current and recent graduates, but well worth using if you are entitled to do so. The psychometric testing section has information about the Saville and Holdsworth GAP series, the MBTI, the OPQ, the civil service selection test and some tests set by individual employers.

The Fulbright Commission

The organization that administers the GMAT tests in the UK. Although these tests are designed for people who wish to study in the USA, the practice material may be of some interest. You can purchase practice books and CD-Roms from the Fulbright Commission in London.

Contact: The Fulbright Commission
Address: 62 Doughty Street
                 London WC1N 2JZ
Tel: 020 7404 6994
Website: www.fulbright.co.uk

Test publishers

All have their own websites and these contain a range of valuable information, including advice for employers about which tests may suit which situations. Websites develop all the time, so check them all for information on helplines, advice to candidates and sample practice material. Some of the major test publishers in the UK are:

Contact: Assessment for Selection and Employment (ASE)
Address: The Chiswick Centre
                 414 Chiswick High Road
                 London W4 5TF
Tel: 020 8996 3337
Website: www.ase-solutions.co.uk

Contact: The Morrisby Organisation
Address: 81 High Street
                 Hemel Hempstead
                 Hertfordshire HP1 3AH
Tel: 01442 215 521
Website: www.morrisby.co.uk

Contact: Oxford Psychologists Press Ltd (OPP)
Address: Lambourne House
                   311-321 Banbury Road
                   Oxford OX2 7JH
Tel: 01865 510203
Website: www.opp.co.uk

Contact: The Psychological Corporation Ltd
Address: 24–28 Oval Road
                   London NW1 7DX
Tel: 020 7424 4200
Website: www.psychcorp.com

Contact: Psytech International Ltd
Address: The Grange
                   Church Road
                   Pullox Hill
                   Bedfordshire MK45 5HE
Tel: 01525 720003
Website: www.psytech.co.uk

Contact: Saville and Holdsworth
Address: The Pavilion
                   1 Atwell Place
                   Thames Ditton
                   Surrey KT7 0NE
Tel: 0870 070 8000
Website: www.shlgroup.com

Contact: The Test Agency Limited
Address: Cray House
                   Church Road
                   Henley-on-Thames
                   Oxfordshire RG9 4AE
Tel: 01491 413413
Website: www.testagency.co.uk